The Supermarine Spitfire I in the European Theatre of Operations

artwork by Jon Freeman

On Target 'Profiles' No 4
Supermarine Spitfire Mk I -VI
European Theatre of Operations

As an aeroplane, the Spitfire needs no introduction – it is amongst the world's most famous fighters. In fact, we deemed the type so important that we have decided to split our coverage of it over several On Target 'Profiles' – to be published at occasional intervals throughout this series of inspirational colour scheme and markings books.

Starting at the beginning seemed reasonable, and so this first homage to the Spitfire starts with the prototype K5054, and runs through the first production type, the Mk I, to the last of the 'short engined' variants, the Mk VI – in RAF service, operating from the UK in what became the European Theatre of Operations.

Future books will cover all the other Marks and sub-types, again split in to suitably-sized references, covering all the Theatres of Operations and including all nationalities.

On Target 'Profiles'

On Target 'Profiles' are designed to complement your existing camouflage and markings reference material. They are not designed to be the 'last word' on the subject, but to act as sources of inspiration – for aircraft modellers and aviation enthusiasts alike.

All the artwork, in this and all the other titles in this series, (provided by a dedicated group of like-minded aviation enthusiast and aircraft modeller artists), is based upon a mixture of contemporary photographs and information from a variety of sources, to offer as wide a ranging coverage as possible, with good quality, well presented and well-researched colour scheme and markings details for specific aircraft types.

On Target 'Profiles' are also an integral part of a bigger package, comprising these and other modeller-friendly reference books, together with exclusive Model Alliance decal sheets and conversion sets in 1:144, 1:72 and 1:48 scales.

ON TARGET 'PROFILES'
are published by
THE AVIATION WORKSHOP PUBLICATIONS LTD
Brook Barn, Letcombe Regis, Wantage, Oxfordshire
OX12 9JD United Kingdom
(part of the Model Alliance Group)
Directors
Gary Madgwick and Neil Robinson
Editorial Consultant Paul Lucus
Printed in the UK by PHP Litho Printers Ltd
Hoyle Mill, Barnsley
South Yorkshire S71 1HN

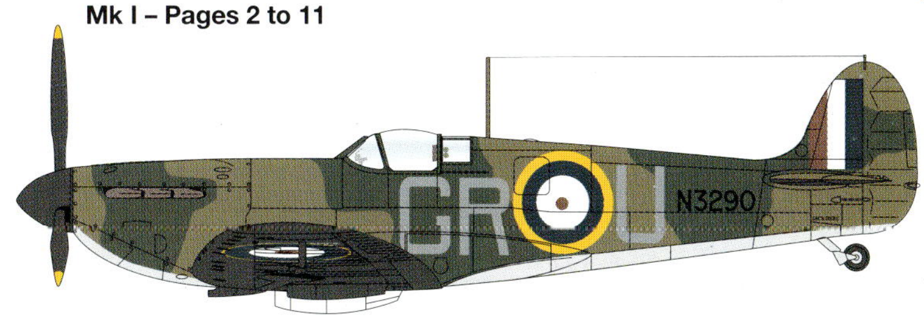

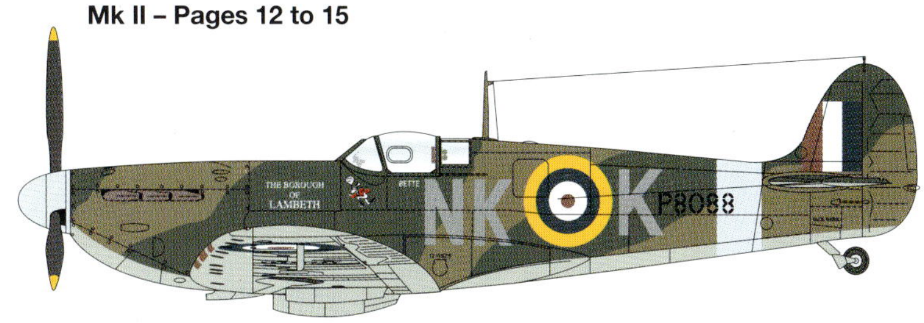

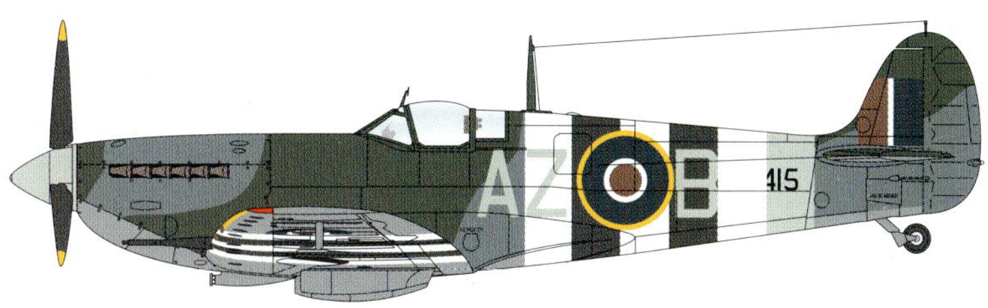

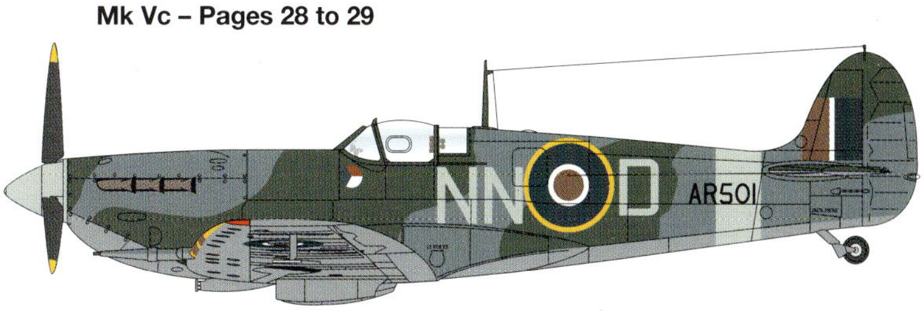

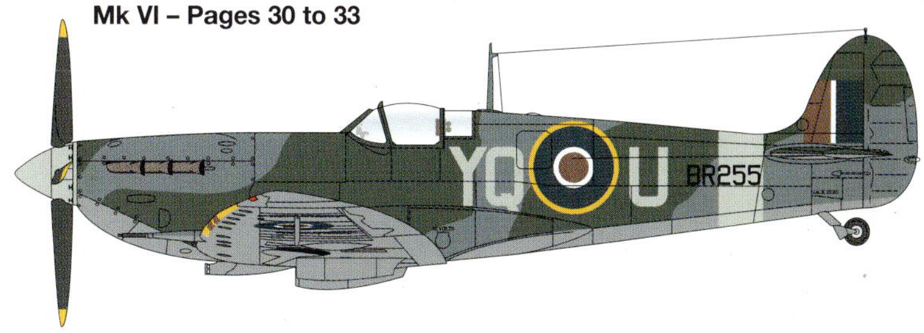

Spitfire Mk.I

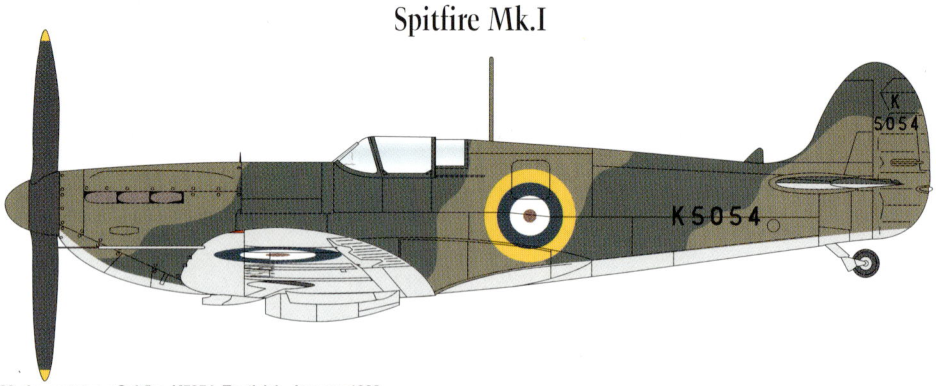

Supermarine Type 300, the prototype Spitfire, K5054, Eastleigh, January 1938
As mentioned in the Inside Front Cover caption, the prototype Spitfire went through a variety of modification standards and colour schemes during its lengthy development and flight trials. Here we have illustrated K5054 as she looked in January 1938, whilst undergoing manufacturers performance trials, armed with eight 0.303 inch machine guns, and fitted with ejector exhaust manifolds and the shackle for the spin recovery parachute on the rear fuselage just infront of the fin. In late September 1937, K5054 had been finished in the relatively newly introduced Temperate Land Scheme upper surfaces of Dark Earth and Dark Green, in what was designed as the 'A' Scheme. Under surfaces were in painted Aluminium. Upperwing roundels were 56 inch diameter Red/White/Blue/Yellow, (see the 4-view on page 3 opposite), with 50 inch diameter Red/White/Blue roundels under the wings. Fuselage roundels were 35 inch diameter Red/White/Blue/Yellow, positioned slightly lower than on subsequent production machines. The serial number on the rear fuselage appears to have been positioned slightly lower than previously and in approximately 6 inch high Night characters. The serial number was also retained on the rudder, again in slightly smaller characters, approximately 4 inches high in Night. 12 inch high Night serials may have been applied under the mainplane at this time – reading from the front under the port wing and from the rear under the starboard wing, (see the 4-view on page 3 opposite). Note the Dark Earth spinner cap.

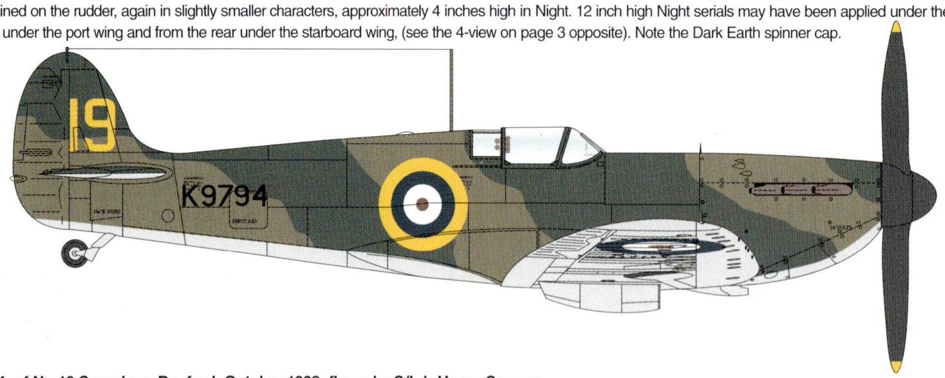

Spitfire Mk I, K9794, of No 19 Squadron, Duxford, October 1938, flown by S/Ldr Henry Cozens
No 19 Squadron had the privilege of being the first RAF Fighter Squadron to be equipped with the Spitfire. Finished in the Temperate Land Scheme upper surfaces of Dark Earth and Dark Green, (in the B Scheme), K9794 had painted Aluminium under surfaces. Upperwing roundels were 56 inch diameter Red/White/Blue/Yellow, (see the 4-view on page 3 opposite), with 50 inch diameter Red/White/Blue roundels under the wings. Fuselage roundels were 35 inch diameter Red/White/Blue/Yellow. 8 inch high Night serial number on the rear fuselage, repeated in 12 inch high Night characters under the mainplane – reading from the front under the port wing and from the rear under the starboard wing, (see the 4-view on page 3 opposite). The Squadron number (19) appeared in Yellow, approximately 20 inch high, numerals on both sides of the fin. Note the standard Night spinner cap.

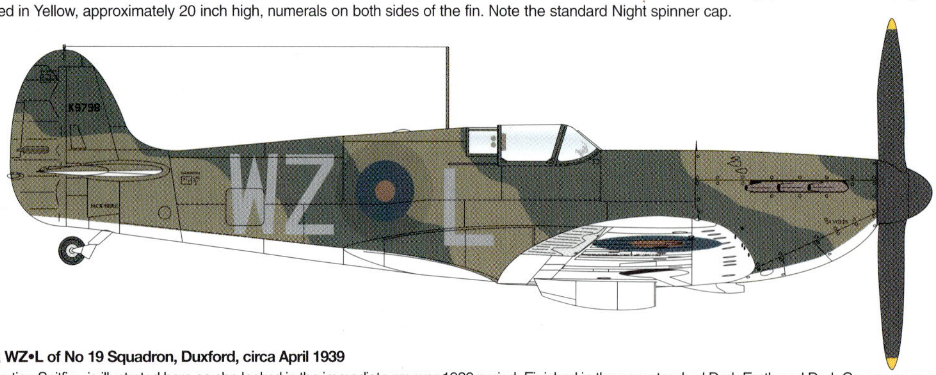

Spitfire Mk I, K9798, WZ•L of No 19 Squadron, Duxford, circa April 1939
K9798, the 11th production Spitfire, is illustrated here as she looked in the immediate pre-war 1939 period. Finished in the now standard Dark Earth and Dark Green upper surfaces, (in the B Scheme), the Aluminium under surfaces were overpainted in Night (port) and White (starboard), divided centrally down the fuselage centreline, following the Munich Crisis of late 1938, to allow the Observer Corps to identify and track 'friendly fighters'. The ailerons were often kept in the original Aluminium to avoid 'balancing problems', as in K9798's case. At the same time, Red/Blue roundels replaced the Red/White/Blue/Yellow ones above the wings and on the fuselage sides – which on in-service machines were painted over the existing roundels either by increasing the Red and Blue portions and painting over the outer Yellow ring with matching camouflage paint, creating 40 inch diameter Red/Blue roundels above the wings and approximately 25 inch diameter Red/Blue roundels on the fuselage or – as with K9798 and most of 19 Squadron's other Spitfires of this period – increasing the upper wing Red and Blue areas to create a 56 inch diameter Red/Blue roundel. Underwing roundels were no longer to be carried, but occasionally, as in K9798's case, the order was misunderstood and they were converted in to 50 inch diameter Red/Blue ones. Also at this time, Squadron code letters were introduced – to be painted in Medium Sea Grey in 48 inch high characters, although smaller letters were permissible depending on the space available on the fuselage, K9798's were approximately 30 inches high. The 8 inch high Night serial number on the rear fuselage was overpainted and re-applied in approximately 2 to 3 inch high Night characters on the fin. Standard Night spinner cap.

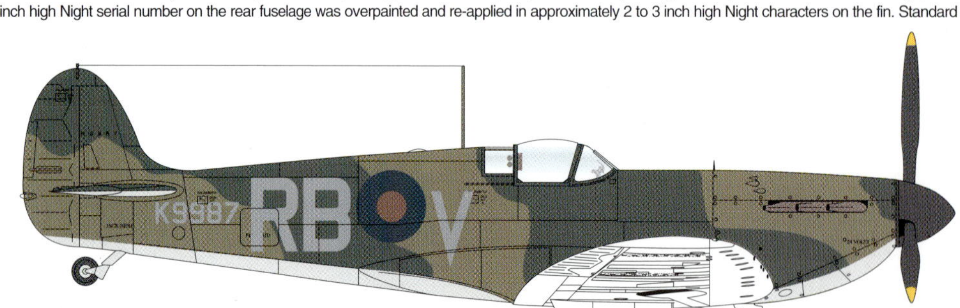

Spitfire Mk I, K9987, RB•V of No 66 Squadron, Duxford, circa April 1939
No 66 was the second RAF Fighter Squadron to receive the Spitfire. K9987 was finished in Dark Earth and Dark Green upper surfaces, (in the B Scheme), with the under surfaces of the Aluminium *mainplanes* only overpainted in Night (port) and White (starboard), divided centrally down the centreline. The ailerons were painted Night/White as appropriate in this instance. The underside of the nose, rear fuselage and the tailplanes remained in Aluminium. 40 inch diameter Red/Blue roundels above the wings with 25 inch diameter Red/Blue roundels on the fuselage. Underwing roundels were not carried. Squadron code letters were approximately 30 inches high in Medium Sea Grey. The serial number on the rear fuselage was overpainted in Medium Sea Grey and also repeated in approximately 2 inch high Night characters on the fin. Note the domed canopy hood and three-blade variable pitch de Havilland propeller and Night spinner – both improvements being introduced on to the Spitfire fleet at this time.

Spitfire Mk.I

Spitfire Mk I, K9797, of No 19 Squadron, Duxford, October 1938
Finished in the Temperate Land Scheme upper surfaces of Dark Earth and Dark Green, in this case in the A Scheme, with Aluminium under surfaces. Upperwing roundels were 56 inch diameter Red/White/Blue/Yellow, with 35 inch diameter Red/White/Blue/Yellow fuselage roundels and 50 inch diameter Red/White/Blue roundels under the wings. 8 inch high Night serial numbers were carried on the rear fuselage, repeated in 12 inch high Night characters under the mainplane – reading from the front under the port wing and from the rear under the starboard wing. The Squadron number (19) appeared in Red, approximately 20 inch high, numerals on both sides of the fin. These were applied, (it is thought in the Squadron's Flight colours), for a series of official photographs, (taken on 31 October 1938 from a Blenheim), and were removed shortly afterwards. Note the Night spinner cap.

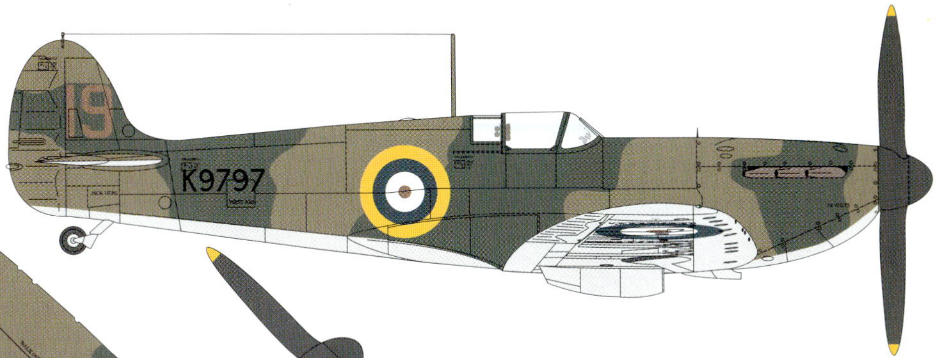

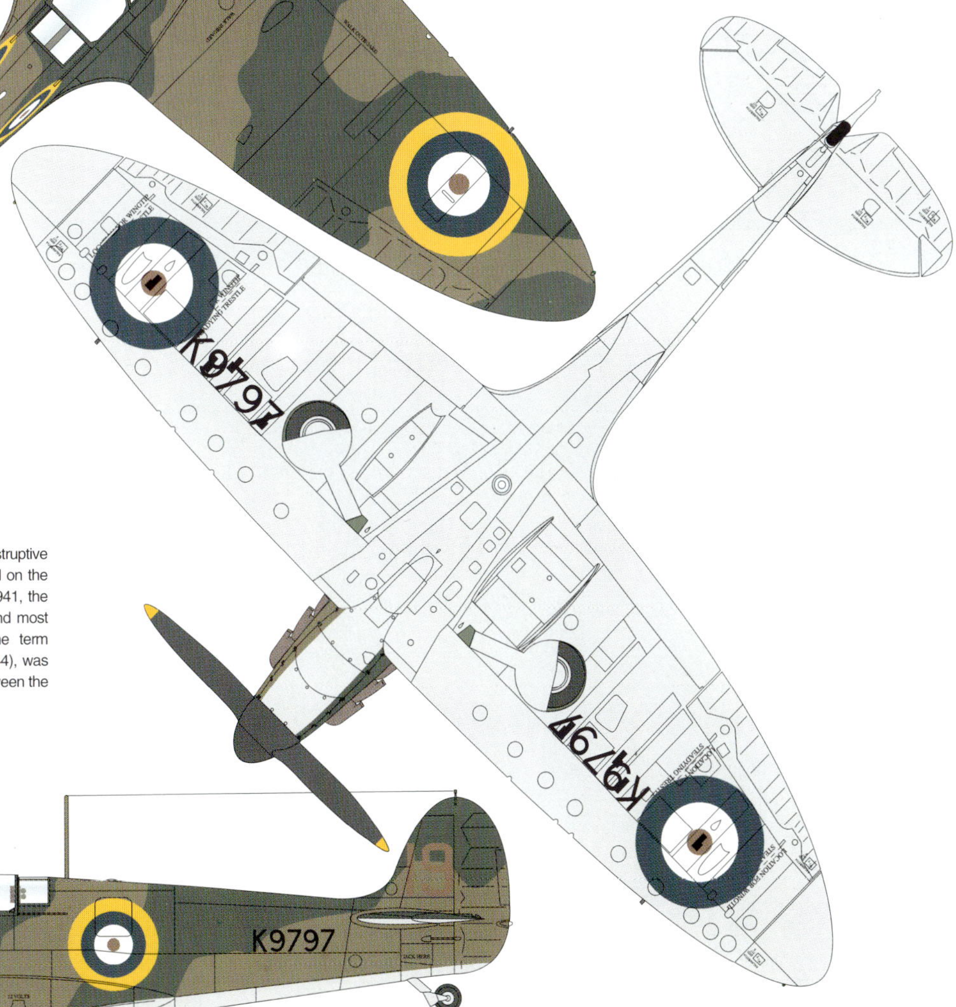

Note: The terms A Scheme or B Scheme refer to the distruptive colour scheme pattern on the upper surfaces, applied on the production line, on alternating airframes. In March 1941, the alternating A and B Scheme system was dropped and most manufacturers opted to apply the A Scheme. The term 'Pattern', (a term introduced by DTD Tech Circular 144), was used to define the relationship of the demarcation between the upper surfaces and under surfaces.

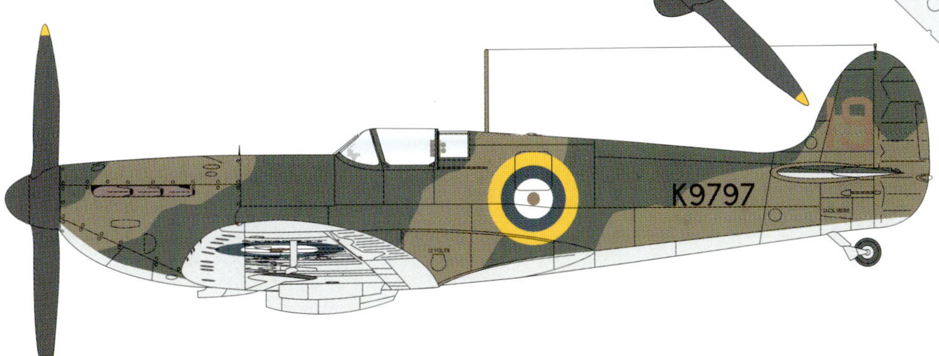

Spitfire Mk.I

Spitfire Mk I, (serial overpainted), SD•H of No 72 Squadron, Church Fenton, circa June 1939
Finished in Dark Earth and Dark Green upper surfaces, (in the B Scheme), the under surfaces were in Night (port) and White (starboard), divided centrally down the centreline. 40 inch diameter Red/Blue roundels above the wings with 25 inch diameter Red/Blue roundels on the fuselage. Underwing roundels were not carried. Squadron code letters were approximately 26 inches high in Medium Sea Grey. The serial number on the rear fuselage was overpainted in matching camouflage colours and is annoyingly unknown at the time of illustration. Note the white, Fighter Squadron, 'spearhead' on the fin, the flat canopy hood and three-blade variable pitch de Havilland propeller and standard Night spinner.

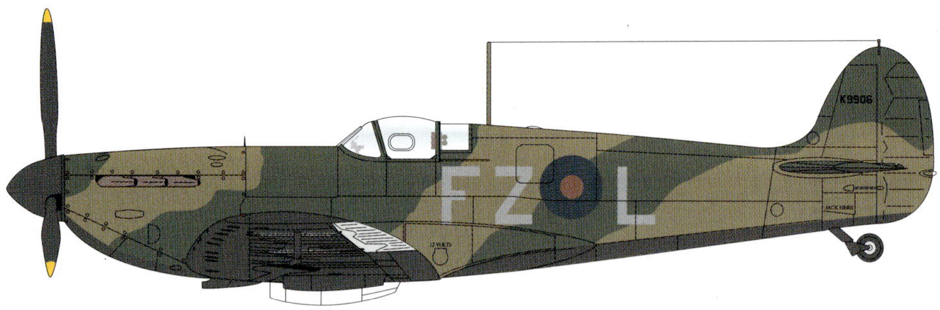

Spitfire Mk I, K9906, FZ•L of No 65 Squadron, Hornchurch, circa August 1939, flown by (the then) F/Lt Robert Stanford Tuck
Finished in Dark Earth and Dark Green upper surfaces, (in the A Scheme), the under surfaces were in Night (port) and White (starboard), divided centrally down the centreline. The ailerons remained in Aluminium. 40 inch diameter Red/Blue roundels above the wings with 25 inch diameter Red/Blue roundels on the fuselage. Underwing roundels were not carried. Squadron code letters were approximately 20 inches high in Medium Sea Grey. The serial number on the rear fuselage had been overpainted and re-applied in approximately 2 to 3 inch high Night characters on the fin. Note the domed canopy hood and three-blade variable pitch de Havilland propeller and standard Night spinner.

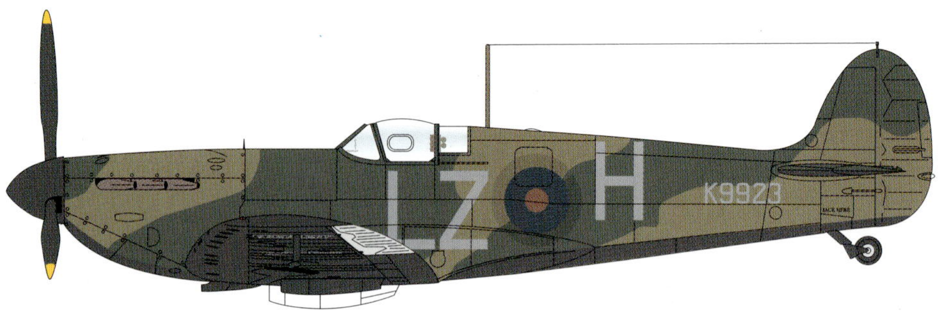

Spitfire Mk I, K9923, LZ•H of No 66 Squadron, Duxford, circa September 1939
This is how the majority of the RAF's Spitfires looked at the outbreak of World War Two. Finished in Dark Earth and Dark Green upper surfaces, (in the A Scheme), the under surfaces were in Night (port) and White (starboard), divided centrally down the centreline. The ailerons remained in Aluminium. 56 inch diameter Red/Blue roundels above the wings with 25 inch diameter Red/Blue roundels on the fuselage. Underwing roundels were not carried. Squadron code letters were approximately 30 inches high in Medium Sea Grey. The 8 inch high serial number on the rear fuselage had been overpainted in Medium Sea Grey. Note the domed canopy hood and three-blade variable pitch de Havilland propeller and standard Night spinner.

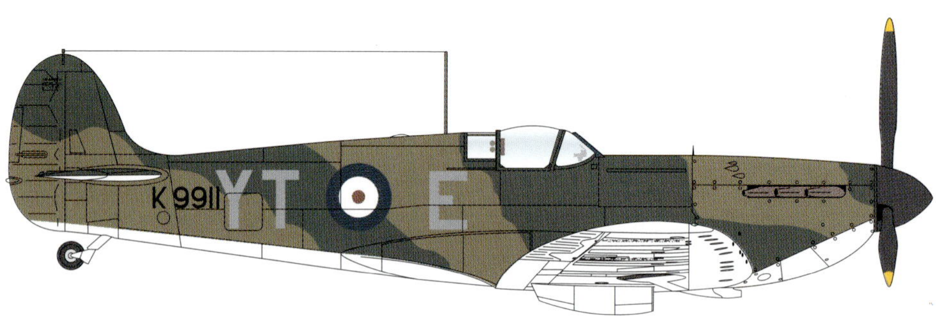

Spitfire Mk I, K9911, YT•E of No 65 Squadron, Hornchurch, late February 1940
By the beginning of 1940, Red/White/Blue fuselage roundels were being introduced as illustrated here on K9911, finished in Dark Earth and Dark Green upper surfaces, (in the B Scheme). The under surfaces were still in Night (port) and White (starboard), divided centrally down the centreline with the ailerons painted Night/White as appropriate. 40 inch diameter Red/Blue roundels were carried above the wings with 25 inch diameter Red/White/Blue roundels on the fuselage. Underwing roundels were not applied. Squadron code letters were approximately 24 inches high in Medium Sea Grey. The 8 inch high serial number was in Night on the rear fuselage. Note the domed canopy hood and three-blade variable pitch de Havilland propeller and standard Night spinner.

Spitfire Mk.I

Spitfire Mk I, N3290, GR•U of No 92 Squadron, Hornchurch, May/June 1940

The first operational Spitfires to land in France were three machines from No 92 Squadron, which had escorted British Prime Minister Winston Churchill's de Havilland Flamingo to Le Bourget, near Paris, on 16 May 1940, for a meeting with his French 'opposite number'. At least one of the aircraft involved, N3290 illustrated here, was finished in the standard Dark Earth and Dark Green upper surfaces, (in the B Scheme), with Night (port) and White (starboard) mainplanes, divided centrally down the centreline, with the underside of the nose, rear fuselage and the tailplanes in Aluminium. 56 inch diameter Red/Blue roundels were carried above the wings. The standard, factory applied, 35 inch diameter, Red/White/Blue fuselage roundel, (with a 5 inch diameter Red centre), had been modified, following an Air Ministry Signal, X485 dated 1 May 1940, for the addition of a Yellow outer ring to be applied to fuselage roundels, (which in N3290's case partially overlapped the Blue ring creating a very non-standard dimension roundel). At the same time, Red/White/Blue 'fin stripes' had been applied, in N3290's case in approximately 7 inch wide bands – the width of the fin stripes had not been specified in the Signal. Red/White/Blue underwing roundels were also ordered to be applied to home-based Day Fighters operating over the Channel or the French mainland, (they had already been carried by all RAF aircraft based on the French mainland since the previous November), with the addition of a Yellow outer ring, *"of convenient width, not less than a quarter nor greater than the full width, of the Blue ring"*, to the roundel under the Night (port) wing. Squadron code letters were approximately 30 inches high in Medium Sea Grey. The Night 8 inch high serial number was in the usual place on the rear fuselage, with the individual aircraft letter in Night, repeated approximately 8 inches high under the nose. Note the gas warning detection square on the port wing upper surface, the domed canopy hood, (now a standard fitment), and the three-blade variable pitch de Havilland propeller with the standard Night spinner.

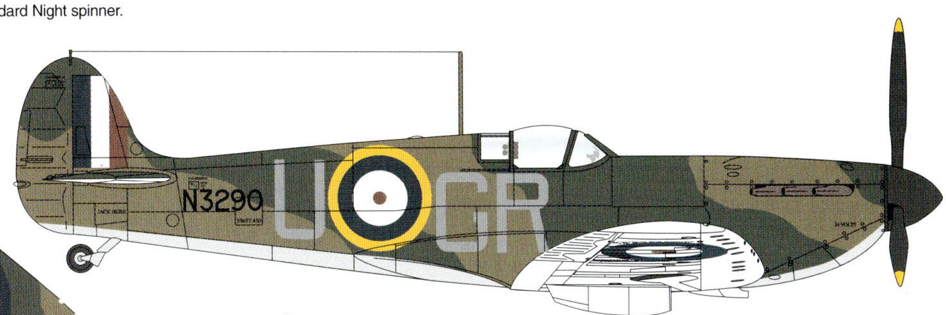

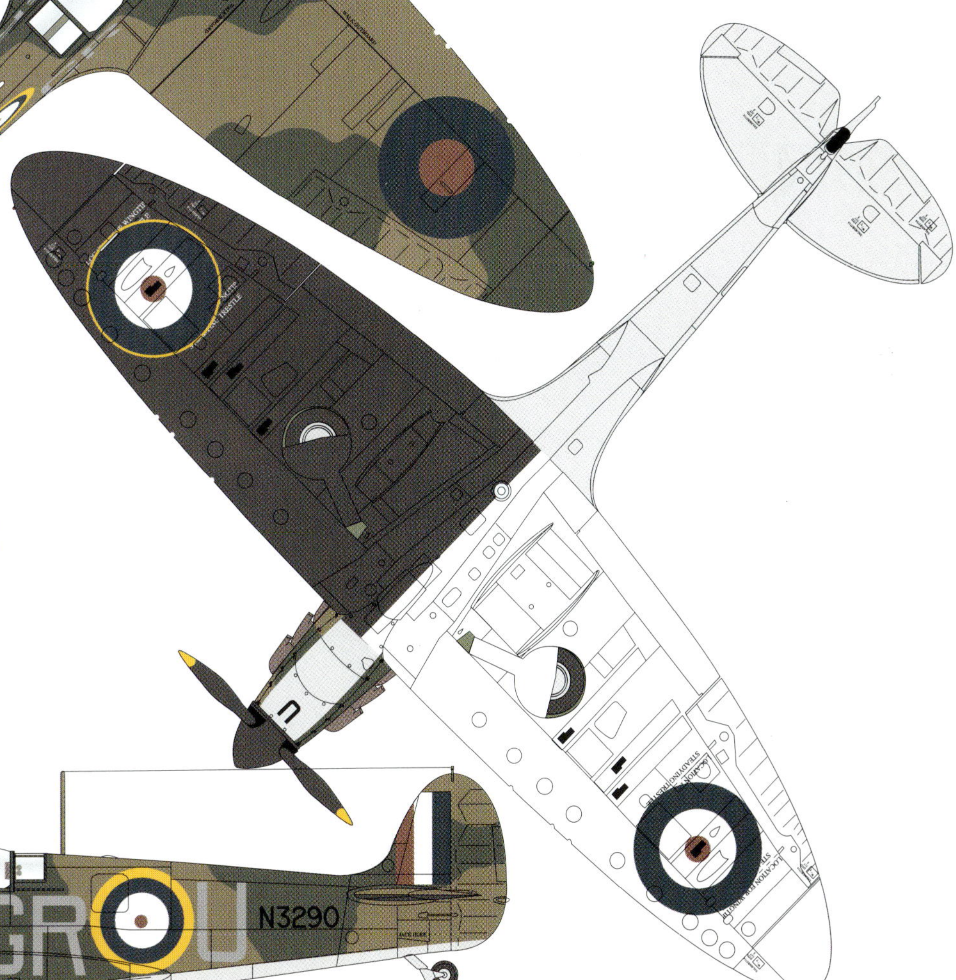

Note: Underwing roundels were introduced on all home-based Fighters following Air Ministry Signal X296, dated 15 May 1940. The Yellow surround to the port underwing roundel was introduced on 4 June 1940, following AM Signal X479.

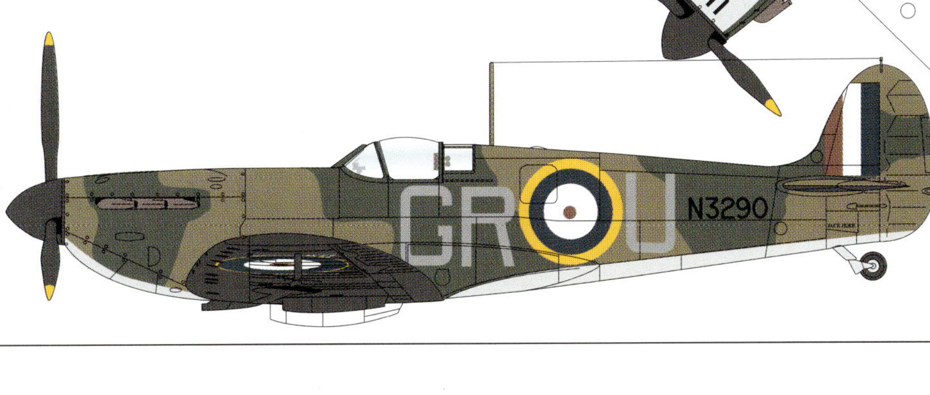

Spitfire Mk.I

Spitfire Mk I, P9372, GR•G of No 92 Squadron, Hornchurch, circa June 1940
Another of No 92 Squadron's Spitfires which was operational over the French mainland during the Dunkirk evacuation. Finished in the standard Dark Earth and Dark Green upper surfaces, (in the A Scheme), with Night (port) and White (starboard) mainplanes, divided centrally down the centreline, with the underside of the nose, rear fuselage and the tailplanes in Aluminium. 56 inch diameter Red/Blue roundels were carried above the wings with standard factory applied, 35 inch diameter, Red/White/Blue fuselage roundels, yet to have the additional Yellow outer ring applied. Note the 5 inch diameter Red centre. The Red/White/Blue 'fin stripes' had also not been applied. Red/White/Blue underwing roundels had been applied as ordered for all home-based Day Fighters operating over the Channel or the French mainland, together with the Yellow outer ring to the roundel under the Night (port) wing. Squadron code letters were again approximately 30 inches high in Medium Sea Grey. The Night 8 inch high serial number was in the usual place on the rear fuselage. Note the domed canopy hood, (now a standard fitment), TR9D radio aerial mast and the three-blade variable pitch de Havilland propeller with the standard Night spinner.

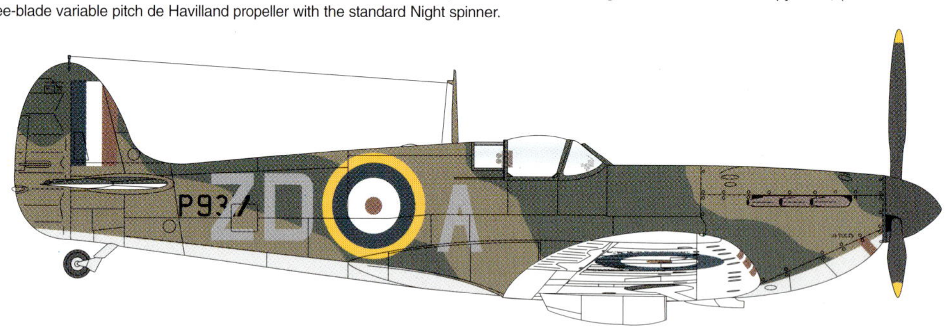

Spitfire Mk I, P9317, ZD•A of No 222 Squadron, Hornchurch, June 1940
Typical of the Spitfires operating over the French mainland during the closing stages of the Battle of France and the Dunkirk evacuation. P9317 was finished in the standard Dark Earth and Dark Green upper surfaces, (in the B Scheme), with Night (port) and White (starboard) mainplanes, divided centrally down the centreline, with the underside of the nose, rear fuselage and the tailplanes in Aluminium. 56 inch diameter Red/Blue roundels were carried above the wings, with the standard, factory applied, 35 inch diameter, Red/White/Blue fuselage roundel, (with a correct 7 inch diameter Red centre), modified with the addition of a Yellow outer ring, (similar to N3290's, on page 5, partially overlapping the Blue ring and creating a very non-standard effect). Red/White/Blue fin stripes had been applied, in approximately 7 inch wide bands. Red/White/Blue underwing roundels were also carried, with the additional Yellow outer ring to the roundel under the Night (port) wing as ordered for home-based Day Fighters operating over the Channel or the French mainland. Squadron code letters were approximately 24 inches high in Medium Sea Grey. The Night 8 inch high serial number was in the usual place on the rear fuselage. Note the Red 'stripe' under the nose, (whose reason is unclear at the time of writing), and the TR9D radio aerial mast. The three-blade variable pitch de Havilland propeller had the standard Night spinner.

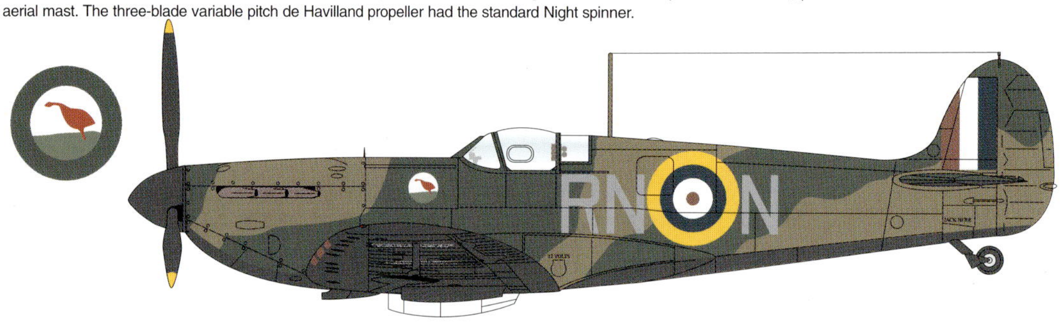

Spitfire Mk I, (serial overpainted), RN•N of No 72 Squadron, Acklington, June 1940
Typical of the home-based Spitfires immediately prior to the Battle of Britain period, RN•N was finished in the standard Dark Earth and Dark Green upper surfaces, (in the A Scheme, with Night (port) and White (starboard) mainplanes, divided centrally down the fuselage centreline. 56 inch diameter Red/Blue roundels were carried above the wings, with a 35 inch diameter, Red/White/Blue/Yellow fuselage roundel, (with a 5 inch diameter Red centre). Red/White/Blue fin stripes had been applied, in approximately 8 inch wide bands. No underwing roundels were carried. Squadron code letters were approximately 22 inches high in Medium Sea Grey. The serial number has been painted out in matching camouflage colours. Note the 'Kiwi' (?) personal motif, exhaust glare shield in front of the windscreen, (fitted for night flying exercises), and the TR9 radio aerial mast. The de Havilland propeller had the standard Night spinner.

Spitfire Mk I, P9398, KL•B of No 54 Squadron, Hornchurch, July 1940, flown by P/O Alan Deere
In June 1940, the Night/White under surfaces of RAF Day Fighters were ordered to be replaced with a new colour called Sky – a pale grey/green shade. However it is thought that due to inadequate supplies of the correct Sky paint, several substitute colours and on-squadron mixes were utilised, resulting in a variety different shades for quite a few months until the supply situation improved. P9398 was finished in the standard Dark Earth and Dark Green upper surfaces, (in the A Scheme), with what is thought to be a 'duck egg green' shade on the under surfaces. 56 inch diameter Red/Blue roundels were carried above the wings with standard 35 inch diameter, Red/White/Blue/Yellow fuselage roundels. Red/White/Blue fin stripes had been applied, in approximately 7 inch wide bands. No underwing roundels were carried. Squadron code letters were approximately 22 inches high in Medium Sea Grey. The Night 8 inch high serial number was in the usual place on the rear fuselage. Note Al Deere's 'Kiwi' personal motif, (which featured on several aircraft that he flew), and the TR9D radio aerial mast. The de Havilland propeller had the standard Night spinner.

Spitfire Mk.I

Spitfire Mk I, P9495, DW•K of No 610 (County of Chester) Squadron, Biggin Hill, July 1940

One of the most illustrated Spitfires of the Battle of Britain period, DW•K has previously been recorded as N3029 which was never on the strength of 610 Sqn., and N3289 which was coded DW•K but was shot down over Dunkirk on 29 May 1940. The aircraft illustrated here, P9495, was operational during June, July and the first few days of August, but was written off with battle damage on 12 August 1940. P9495 was finished in the standard Dark Earth and Dark Green upper surfaces, (in the B Scheme), with what is thought to be a 'duck egg blue' shade on the under surfaces, possibly BS381 No1 Sky Blue, a fairly dark 'duck egg blue' colour. 56 inch diameter Red/Blue roundels were carried above the wings with 35 inch diameter, Red/White/Blue fuselage roundels outlined with an extra ring of Yellow creating a 49 inch diameter Red/White/Blue/Yellow marking. The Red/White/Blue fin stripes were in approximately 6 inch wide bands. No underwing roundels were carried. Squadron code letters were some 33 inches high in Medium Sea Grey. The Night 8 inch high serial number was in the usual place on the rear fuselage, partially overpainted on the starboard side by the code letters. The de Havilland propeller had the standard Night spinner.

Spitfire Mk.I

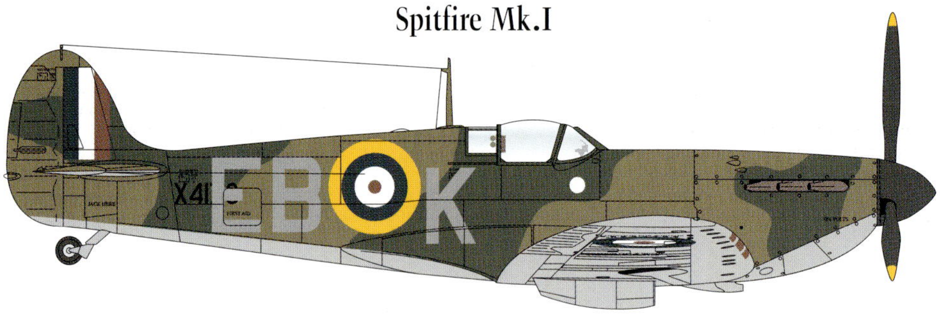

Spitfire Mk I, X4178, EB•K of No 41 Squadron, Hornchurch, August 1940

From 11 August 1940, Red/White/Blue roundels were re-introduced on to the under surfaces of the wings. X4178 was finished in the standard Dark Earth and Dark Green upper surfaces, (in the A Scheme), with what is thought to be a 'pale grey' shade on the under surfaces, possibly an existing colour called Sky Grey. 56 inch diameter Red/Blue roundels were carried above the wings with standard 35 inch diameter, Red/White/Blue/Yellow fuselage roundels. Red/White/Blue fin stripes had been applied, in approximately 7 inch wide bands. Approximately 40 inch diameter Red/White/Blue underwing roundels were carried. Squadron code letters were approximately 30 inches high in Medium Sea Grey. The Night 8 inch high serial number was in the usual place on the rear fuselage and the de Havilland propeller had the standard Night spinner.

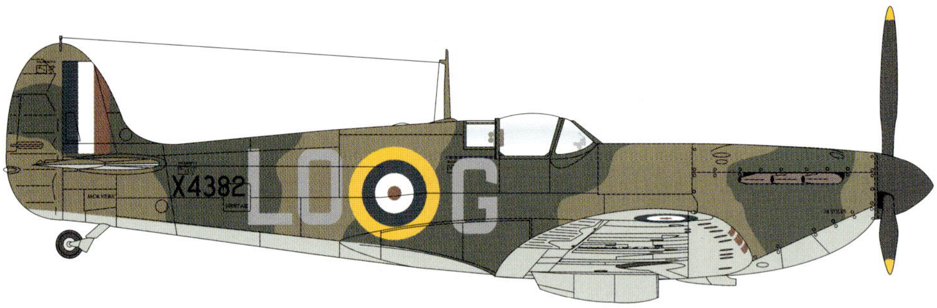

Spitfire Mk I, X4382, LO•G of No 602 (City of Glasgow) Squadron, Westhampnett, August/September 1940, flown by P/O Osgood Hanbury

No 602 Squadron had already been 'blooded' whilst operating from Drem, in Scotland, prior to being sent south to become part of the Tangmere Wing. Finished in the standard Dark Earth and Dark Green upper surfaces, (in the A Scheme), X4382 possibly had the correct shade of Sky applied to its under surfaces by this stage. 56 inch diameter Red/Blue roundels were carried above the wings with standard 35 inch diameter, Red/White/Blue/Yellow fuselage roundels. Red/White/Blue fin stripes had been applied, in approximately 7 inch wide bands. Approximately 25 inch diameter Red/White/Blue underwing roundels were carried. Squadron code letters were approximately 27 inches high in Medium Sea Grey. The Night 8 inch high serial number was in the usual place on the rear fuselage and the de Havilland propeller had the standard Night spinner.

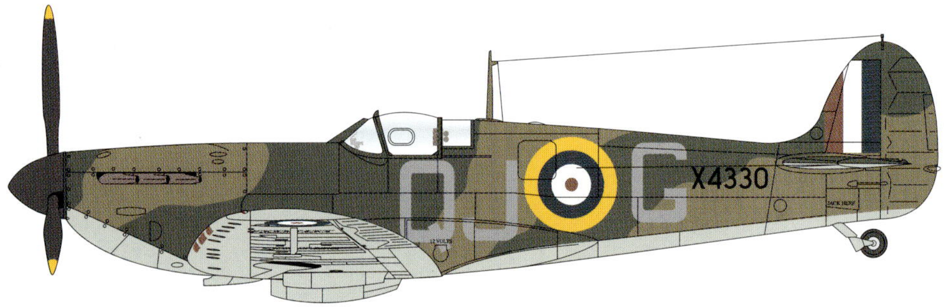

Spitfire Mk I, X4330, QJ•G of No 616 (South Yorkshire) Squadron, Kirton-in-Lindsey, September 1940, thought to have been flown by P/O J E 'Johnnie' Johnson

No 616 Squadron had fought over the beaches of Dunkirk and then from Kenley and Coltishall during August and September, but suffered extensive losses and was sent north to 'rest' in mid-September, where it stayed for the remainder of the Battle of Britain. Finished in the standard Dark Earth and Dark Green upper surfaces, (in the A Scheme), X4330 may also have had the correct shade of Sky applied to its under surfaces by mid/late September. 56 inch diameter Red/Blue roundels were carried above the wings with standard 35 inch diameter, Red/White/Blue/Yellow fuselage roundels. Red/White/Blue fin stripes had been applied, in approximately 7 inch wide bands. Approximately 25 inch diameter Red/White/Blue underwing roundels were carried. Squadron code letters, (still the pre-war allocation of QJ, which was also being used by No 92 Sqn., an anomaly that was not adjusted until mid-1941), were approximately 30 inches high in Medium Sea Grey. The Night 8 inch high serial number was in the usual place on the rear fuselage, (but positioned a little highter), and the de Havilland propeller had the standard Night spinner.

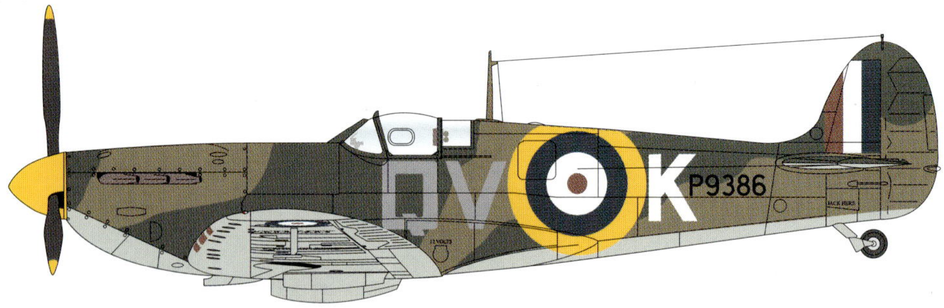

Spitfire Mk I, P9386, QV•K of No 19, Fowlmere, September 1940, flown by S/Ldr Brian Lane

P9386 was finished in the standard Dark Earth and Dark Green upper surfaces, (in the A Scheme), and probably had the correct shade of Sky applied to its under surfaces by mid/late September. 56 inch diameter Red/Blue roundels were carried above the wings with 35 inch diameter, Red/White/Blue fuselage roundels modified by the addition of a Yellow outer ring to form a 49 inch diameter Red/White/Blue/Yellow roundel. The Red/White/Blue fin stripes were some 7 inches wide and the full height of the fin. Approximately 25 inch diameter Red/White/Blue underwing roundels were carried at the extreme tips of the wing. Code letters, were approximately 27 inches high, with the Squadron identification letters, QV, in Medium Sea Grey and the individual aircraft letter 'K' in either a very pale grey or white. The Night 8 inch high serial number was in the usual place on the rear fuselage. The de Havilland propeller's spinner was a very non-standard colour, which is thought to have been Yellow.

Spitfire Mk.I

Spitfire Mk I, N3093, QJ•W of No 616 (South Yorkshire) Squadron, Leconfield, August 1940, flown by F/Lt Denys Gillam

N3093 is illustrated as she looked in mid-August 1940, finished in the standard Dark Earth and Dark Green upper surfaces, (in the B Scheme pattern), with a unit applied 'pale blue' shade on the under surfaces. 56 inch diameter Red/Blue roundels were carried above the wings with standard 35 inch diameter, Red/White/Blue/Yellow fuselage roundels. Red/White/Blue fin stripes had been applied, in approximately 7 inch wide bands. No underwing roundels had yet been applied. Squadron code letters, (still in the pre-war allocation of QJ, which was also being used by No 92 Sqn., an anomaly that was not adjusted until mid-1941), were approximately 24 inches high in Medium Sea Grey. The Night 8 inch high serial number was in the usual place on the rear fuselage, but may have been painted over in matching camouflage colours at this time. Note, Denys Gillam's *'The Virgin'* cartoon on the cockpit entry door. The de Havilland propeller had a Night spinner.

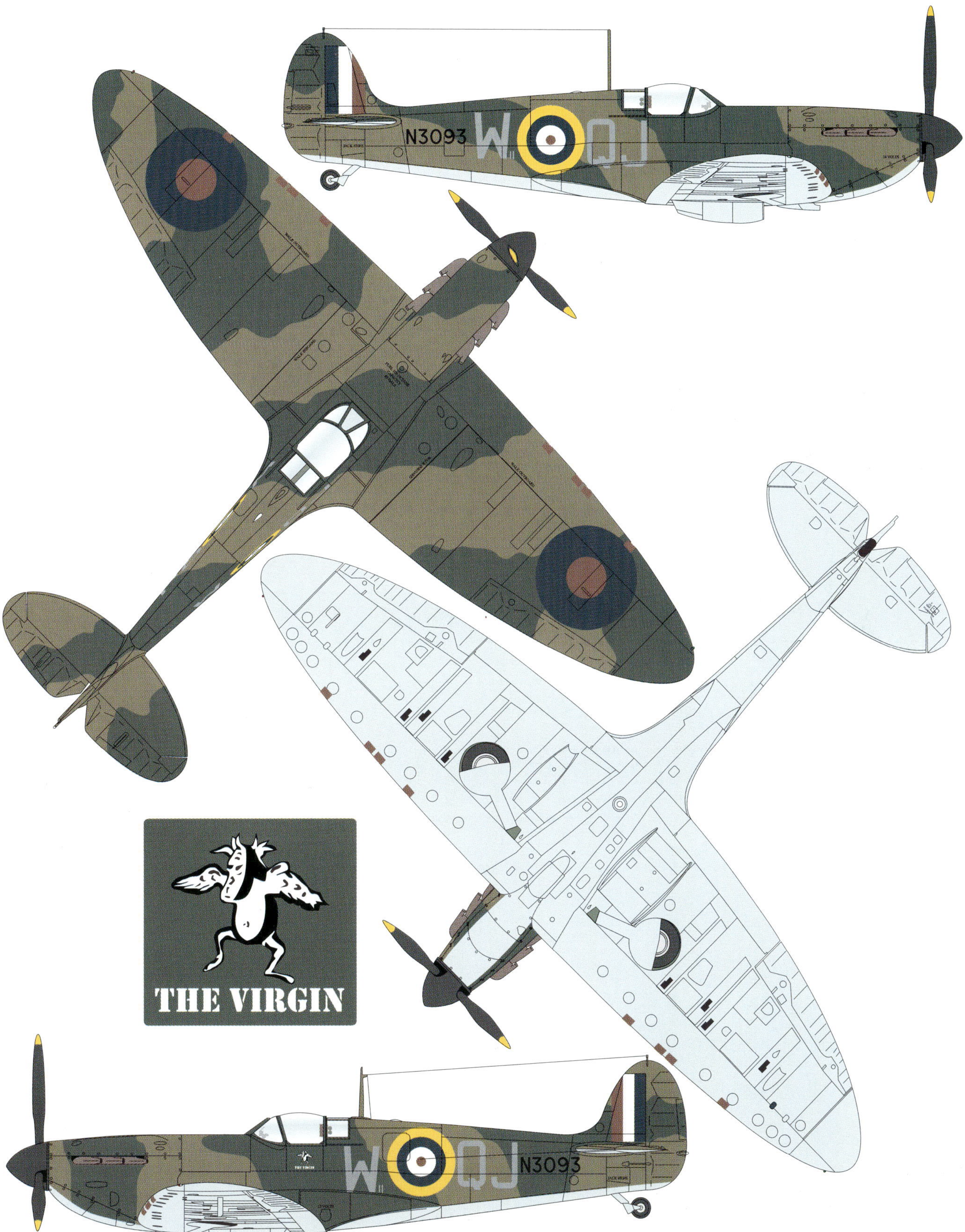

Spitfire Mk.I & Ib

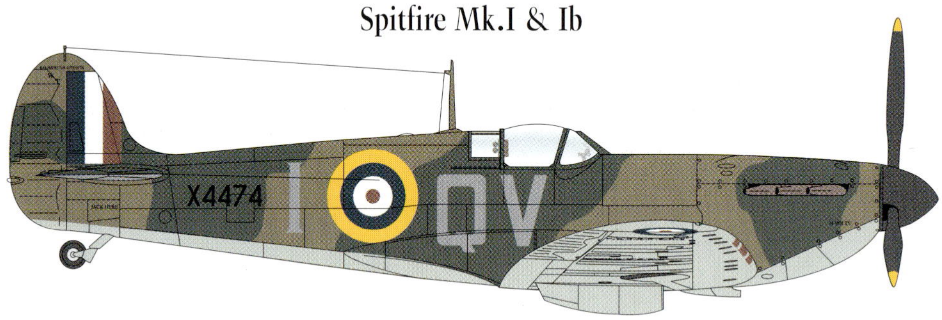

Spitfire Mk I, X4474, QV•I of No19 Squadron, Fowlmere, September 1940, flown by Sqt Bernard Jennings
Typical of the late Battle of Britain period, X4474 was finished in the standard Dark Earth and Dark Green upper surfaces, (in the A Scheme), with what is thought to be the correct shade of Sky under surfaces. 56 inch diameter Red/Blue roundels were carried above the wings with 35 inch diameter, Red/White/Blue/Yellow fuselage roundels. The Red/White/Blue fin stripes were approximately 7 inches wide and extended the full height of the fin. Approximately 25 inch diameter Red/White/Blue underwing roundels were carried at the extreme tips of the wings. Squadron code letters were approximately 27 inches high in Medium Sea Grey. Note the presentation of the individual aircraft letter 'I' with serifs at the top and the bottom. The Night 8 inch high serial number was in the usual place on the rear fuselage and the de Havilland propeller had a Night spinner.

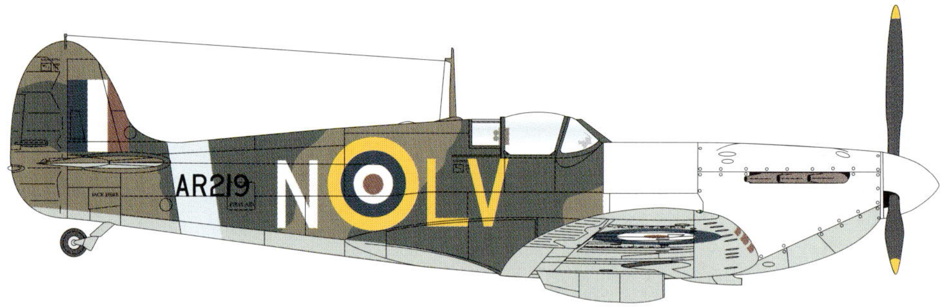

Spitfire Mk I, AR219, LV•N of No 57 Operational Training Unit, Hawarden, circa mid-1941
AR219 was a late production Mk I, built by Westland, used by the instructors at No 57 OTU as a 'bounce' aircraft. It was finished in standard Dark Earth and Dark Green upper surfaces, (in the A Scheme), with Sky under surfaces. The undersides of the port wing may have been overpainted in temporary, Special Night distemper. The entire upper surfaces of the nose area had been overpainted in white has had the de Havilland propeller spinner. 56 inch diameter Red/Blue roundels were carried above the wings with 35 inch diameter, Red/White/Blue/Yellow fuselage roundels. Note the 7 inch diameter Red centre spot – a frequent anomaly found on several Spitfire Mk Is and IIs. The Red/White/Blue fin stripes were each 8 inches wide and extended 27 inches in height. Approximately 50 inch diameter Red/White/Blue underwing roundels were carried; the one under the port wing was possibly outlined in Yellow. Unit code letters were approximately 27 inches high in Yellow with the individual aircraft letter in white or very pale grey. The rear Sky Blue fuselage tail band marking, introduced in November 1940, was initially applied at unit or MU level, (rather than on the production line at the manufacturers), and consequently sometimes varied in presentation. Ostensibly to be 18 inches wide, in AR219's instance it followed the fuselage transportation break joint line rather than being 'vertical' to the datum line of the fuselage. The Night 8 inch high serial number was in the usual place on the rear fuselage.

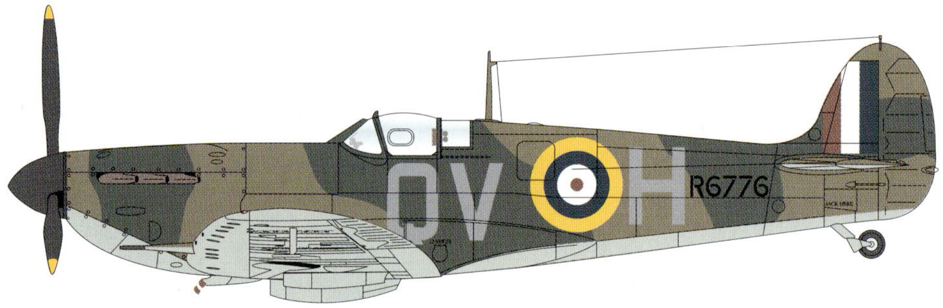

Spitfire Mk I (cannon-armed), R6776, QV•H of No 19 Squadron, Fowlmere, circa August 1940, flown by Flt/Sgt George Unwin
R6776 was one of the first Spitfire Mk Is to be trial-fitted with Hispano/BSA 20mm cannons, which initially proved unsatisfactory due to persistent stoppages caused by the flexing of the wing in high-G manoevres. The aircraft were withdrawn from service at the end of August and fitted with an improved feed mechanism which cured the problem and were subsequently re-issued to No 92 Squadron – (see below and opposite) – under the Mk Ib designation. In July/August, R6776 was finished in standard Dark Earth and Dark Green upper surfaces, (in the B Scheme), with Sky under surfaces. 56 inch diameter Red/Blue roundels were carried above the wings with 35 inch diameter, Red/White/Blue/Yellow fuselage roundels. The Red/White/Blue fin stripes were each approximately 7 inches wide and extended the full height of the fin. Underwing roundels were not carried during this period. Squadron code letters were approximately 30 inches high in Medium Sea Grey. The Night 8 inch high serial number was in the usual place on the rear fuselage and the de Havilland propeller had a Night spinner.

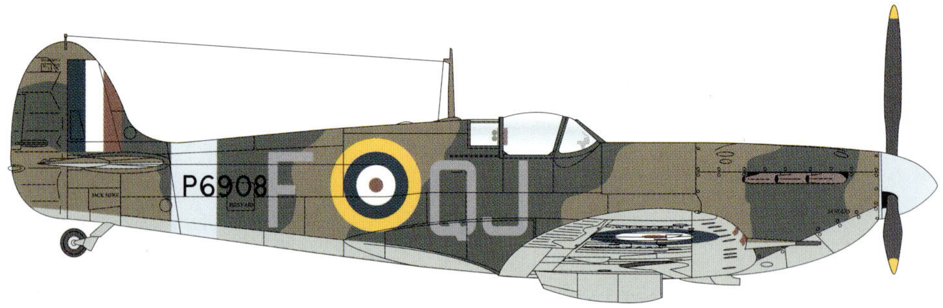

Spitfire Mk Ib, R6908, QJ•F of No 92 Squadron, Biggin Hill, circa December 1940
R6908, one of the first production Hispano/BSA 20mm cannon-armed Spitfire Mk Ibs, was finished in standard Dark Earth and Dark Green upper surfaces, (in the A Scheme), with Sky under surfaces. The under surface of the port wing was painted in the temporary, Special Night distemper introduced in November 1940. 56 inch diameter Red/Blue roundels were carried above the wings with 35 inch diameter, Red/White/Blue/Yellow fuselage roundels. The Red/White/Blue fin stripes were each approximately 7 inches wide and extended the full height of the fin. 50 inch diameter underwing roundels were carried, the one under the port wing being thinly outlined in Yellow. Squadron code letters were approximately 30 inches high in Medium Sea Grey. The 18 inch wide rear fuselage identification band had been applied in Sky Blue and the de Havilland propeller had a Sky Blue spinner. The 8 inch high Night serial number was in the usual place on the rear fuselage and had been re-applied over the Sky Blue band where appropriate.

Spitfire Mk.Ib

Spitfire Mk Ib, X4272, QJ•D of No 92 Squadron, Biggin Hill, circa December 1940

No 92 Squadron was chosen as the Service Trials Unit for the production Hispano/BSA 20mm cannon-armed Spitfire Mk I, (designated as the Mk Ib), now fitted with the improved armament feed mechanism. X4272, delivered in early December, was finished in standard Dark Earth and Dark Green upper surfaces, (in the A Scheme), with Sky under surfaces. The under surface of the port wing was painted in the temporary, Special Night distemper introduced in November 1940 as an aid to tracking 'friendly' fighters combating the Luftwaffe's high altitude fighter-bomber raids. 56 inch diameter Red/Blue roundels were carried above the wings with 35 inch diameter, Red/White/Blue/Yellow fuselage roundels. The Red/White/Blue fin stripes were each approximately 7 inches wide and extended the full height of the fin. 25 inch diameter underwing roundels were carried at the extreme tips – applied by 6 MU in August prior to delivery to No 92 – the one under the port wing being thinly outlined in Yellow. Squadron code letters were approximately 30 inches high in Medium Sea Grey. The 18 inch wide rear fuselage identification band, introduced at the same time as the Night port underwing, had been applied in Sky Blue and the de Havilland propeller had a Sky Blue spinner. It is believed that well in to 1941, the tail bands and spinners were painted in this Sky Blue shade, (specifically Air Ministry Sky Blue), which helps to explain the difference in tone between the 'Sky' bands and spinners and Sky under surfaces on the same aircraft. The 8 inch high Night serial number was in the usual place on the rear fuselage and had been re-applied over the Sky Blue band where appropriate.

Spitfire Mk.IIa

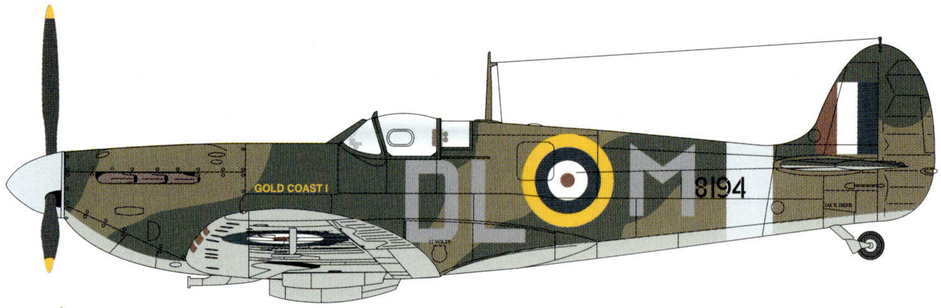

Spitfire Mk IIa, P8194, DL•M of No 91 (Nigeria) Squadron, Hawkinge, circa April/May 1941, flown by F/Lt Don Mackay

No 91 Squadron was formed by re-numbering No 421 Flight in January 1941. P8194, was finished in standard Dark Earth and Dark Green upper surfaces, (in the A Scheme), with Sky under surfaces. 56 inch diameter Red/Blue roundels were carried above the wings with 35 inch diameter, Red/White/Blue/Yellow fuselage roundels. Fin markings were now to be standardised at three Red/White/Blue bands, each 8 inches wide and 27 inches high. Aircraft already in squadron service complied with this order by modifying their existing 'full height' stripes, (in P8194's instance, still 7 inches wide), by overpainting the top of the fin in matching camouflage colours. 50 inch diameter Red/White/Blue underwing roundels were now carried as standard. Squadron code letters were approximately 33 inches high with the individual aircraft letter some 24 inches high – all in Medium Sea Grey. The 18 inch wide rear fuselage band and the de Havilland propeller spinner were still being painted in Sky Blue. The 8 inch high Night serial number was in the usual place on the rear fuselage and had been re-applied over the Sky Blue band where appropriate. Note presentation name *'Gold Coast I'* on cowling.

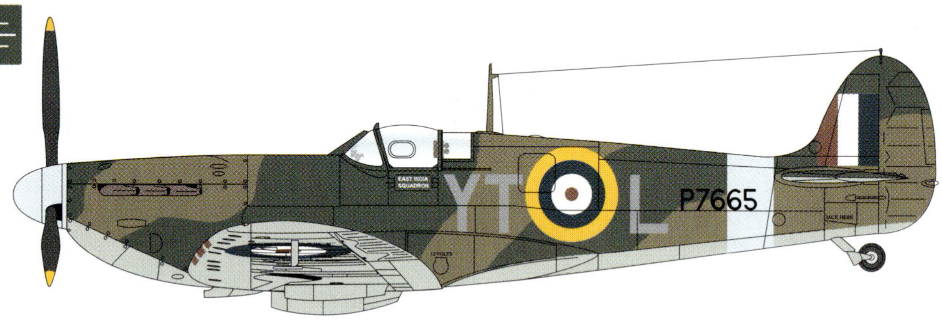

Spitfire Mk IIa, P7665, YT•L of No 65 (East India) Squadron, Kirton-in-Lindsey, circa July 1941

In 1941, No 65, was officially adopted as the first, (of three), 'East India' Squadrons, and sported the appropriate wording under the cockpit canopy. P7665, was finished in standard Dark Earth and Dark Green upper surfaces, (in the A Scheme), with Sky under surfaces. 56 inch diameter Red/Blue roundels were carried above the wings with 35 inch diameter, Red/White/Blue/Yellow fuselage roundels. Fin markings were 7 inches wide and 27 inches high, modified by overpainting the top of the existing 'full height' stripes in matching camouflage colours. 50 inch diameter Red/White/Blue underwing roundels were carried. Squadron code letters were approximately 24 inches high in Medium Sea Grey. The 18 inch wide rear fuselage band and the Rotol propeller spinner were in Sky Blue. The 8 inch high Night serial number was in the usual place on the rear fuselage and had been re-applied over the Sky Blue band where appropriate.

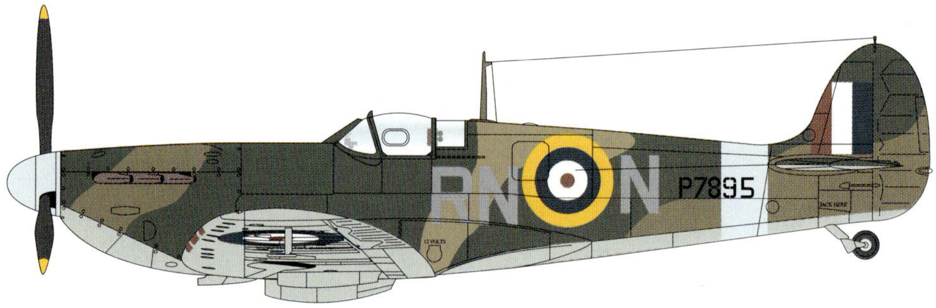

Spitfire Mk IIa, P7895, RN•N of No 72 Squadron, Acklington, circa early summer 1941

P7895, is illustrated here finished in Dark Earth and Dark Green upper surfaces, (in the A Scheme), with Sky under surfaces, immediately prior to the change-over to the 'grey and green' Day Fighter scheme. The colour photograph upon which this illustration is based, shows P7895 in a very weathered and worn condition with quite startling variations in the shades of the Dark Earth and Dark Geen! 56 inch diameter Red/Blue roundels were carried above the wings with 35 inch diameter, Red/White/Blue/Yellow fuselage roundels. Fin markings were 8 inches wide and 27 inches high. 50 inch diameter Red/White/Blue underwing roundels were carried. Squadron code letters were approximately 24 inches high in Medium Sea Grey. The 18 inch wide rear fuselage band and the Rotol propeller spinner were in Sky Blue. The 8 inch high Night serial number was in the usual place on the rear fuselage and had been re-applied over the Sky Blue band where appropriate.

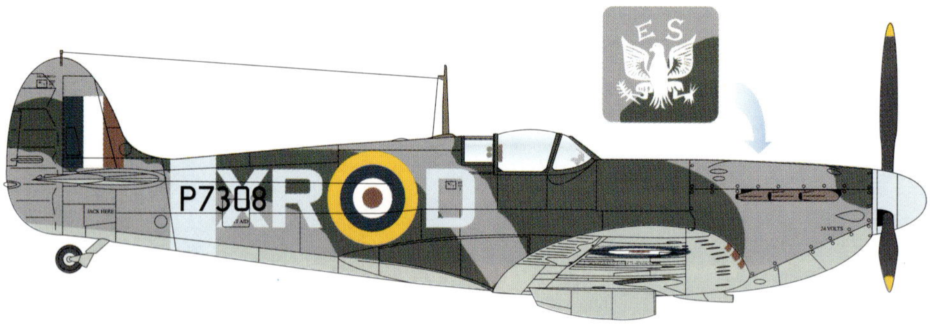

Spitfire Mk IIa, P7308, XR•D of No 71 (Eagle) Squadron, North Weald, August 1941, flown by P/O Bill Dunn

No 71 Squadron was re-formed in September 1940, with American volunteer pilots, (hence the 'Eagle' name), initially briefly equipped with Brewster Buffalos and then Hurricanes, until it received Spitfire Mk IIs in August 1941, with which the unit scored two 'kills', both by Bill Dunn in P7308. The aircraft is shown as it looked on 27 August, (the date on which Bill Dunn despatched the two Bf 109s), finished in an 'on squadron' partial repaint, consisting of Dark Green and a 'lighter' shade of Mixed Grey upper surfaces, (in an approximation of the B Scheme), possibly still with Sky under surfaces, which *should* have been repainted in Medium Sea Grey following the Air Ministry instructions of 15 August 1941. 56 inch diameter Red/Blue roundels were carried above the wings with 35 inch diameter, Red/White/Blue/Yellow fuselage roundels. Fin markings were 8 inches wide and 27 inches high. 50 inch diameter Red/White/Blue underwing roundels were carried. Squadron code letters were approximately 24 inches high, possibly in Sky Blue, as was the 18 inch wide rear fuselage band and the Rotol propeller spinner - all of which should have been repainted inSky. The 8 inch high Night serial number was in the usual place on the rear fuselage and had been re-applied over the tail band and Squadron codes where appropriate.

Spitfire Mk.IIa

Spitfire Mk IIa, P8088, NK•K of No 118 Squadron, Ibsley, May 1941, flown by P/O Alec Lumsden
Following the Battle of Britain, the RAF went over to the offensive, and No 118 was amongst the many RAF Fighter squadrons "*taking the fight back to the enemy*". P8088, a Castle Bromwich-built machine, is typical of how RAF Spitfires were finished in early 1941; still in the Temperate Land Scheme of Dark Earth and Dark Green upper surfaces, (in the A Scheme) which was being standardised upon by most of the manufacturers), with Sky under surfaces. The temporary, Special Night distemper under the port wing was ordered to be removed in mid-April 1941 and the under surfaces on RAF Fighter Command aircraft returned to overall Sky. 56 inch diameter Red/Blue roundels were carried above the wings with 35 inch diameter, Red/White/Blue/Yellow fuselage roundels. Fin markings were 8 inches wide and 27 inches high. 50 inch diameter Red/White/Blue underwing roundels were carried. Squadron code letters were approximately 24 inches high in Medium Sea Grey, with the individual aircraft letter repeated under the nose, approximately 12 inches high, in Night. The 18 inch wide rear fuselage band and the Rotol propeller spinner were still in Sky Blue. The 8 inch high Night serial number was in the usual place on the rear fuselage and had been re-applied over the Sky Blue band where appropriate. Note the presentation name 'The Borough of Lambeth' and the personal name 'Bette' on both sides of the fuselage and the cartoon of Captain A R P Reilly-Foull from the *Daily Mirror* cartoon strip, 'Just Jake' under the port windscreen.

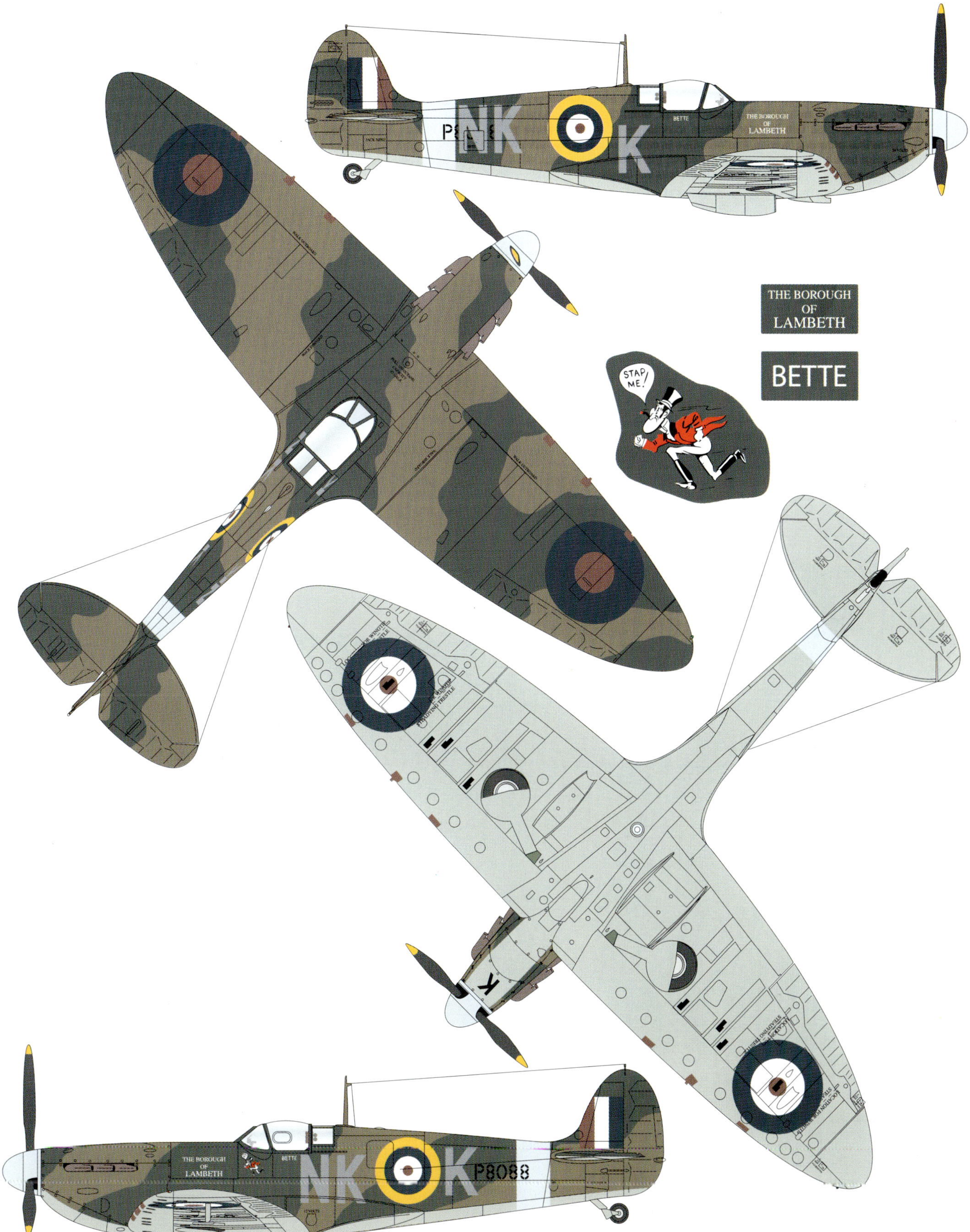

Spitfire Mk.IIa & IIb

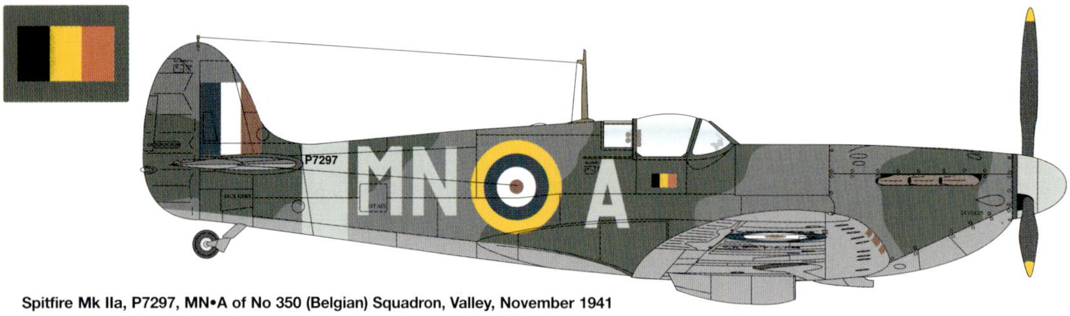

Spitfire Mk IIa, P7297, MN•A of No 350 (Belgian) Squadron, Valley, November 1941
No 350 was the first of the Belgian-manned squadrons, forming at RAF Valley in November 1941, and the Squadron's initial equipment was the Spitfire Mk IIa. The summer and autumn of 1941 also witnessed the replacement of the Dark Earth/Dark Green Temperate Land Scheme upper surfaces for the 'grey/green' Day Fighter Scheme upper surfaces. P7297 is illustrated with 'Mixed Grey' applied over the original Dark Earth areas, but retaining the original Dark Green, (in the A Scheme), with Medium Sea Grey – the new Day Fighter Scheme under surface colour – painted over the original Sky under surfaces. Mixed Grey was produced by mixing seven parts of Medium Sea Grey to one part of Night – at the issuing MU or often at 'on-squadron' level. 56 inch diameter Red/Blue roundels were still carried above the wings, with 35 inch diameter, Red/White/Blue/Yellow fuselage roundels and 50 inch diameter Red/White/Blue underwing roundels. Red/White/Blue fin marking was 24 inches wide and 27 inches high. Squadron code letters were approximately 27 inches high – in Sky. The 18 inch wide rear fuselage band and the Rotol propeller spinner may still have been in Sky Blue although Sky is more probable as illustrated. The serial number had been re-painted over the Sky/Sky Blue band in approximately 3 inch high Night characters. Note the Belgian tri-colour flag under the canopy hood.

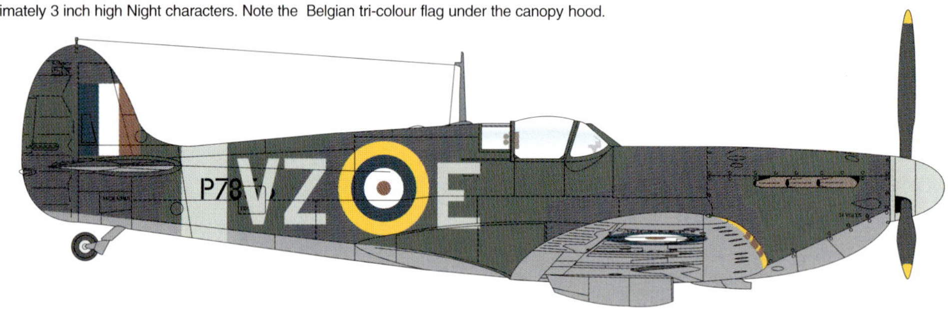

Spitfire Mk IIa, P7856, VZ•E of No 412 (Canadian) Squadron, Digby, October 1941, flown by F/Sgt E N MacDonnell
No 412 was a Canadian-manned unit and received its first Spitfires, (Mk IIs), in June 1941. On 13 October, F/Sgt MacDonnell claimed the squadron's first 'kill' – a Bf 109 – in P7856. P7856 is another example of the overpainting of the original Dark Earth areas of the upper surfaces with Mixed Grey, (in the A Scheme), with Medium Sea Grey under surfaces. Note application of the Yellow wing leading edges, also introduced at this time. 56 inch diameter Red/Blue roundels were carried above the wings, with 35 inch diameter, Red/White/Blue/Yellow fuselage roundels and 50 inch diameter Red/White/Blue roundels under the wings. Red/White/Blue fin marking was 24 inches wide and 27 inches high. Squadron code letters were approximately 24 inches high in Sky. The 18 inch wide rear fuselage band and the Rotol propeller spinner were probably Sky as illustrated. The 8 inch high Night serial number was in the usual place on the rear fuselage.

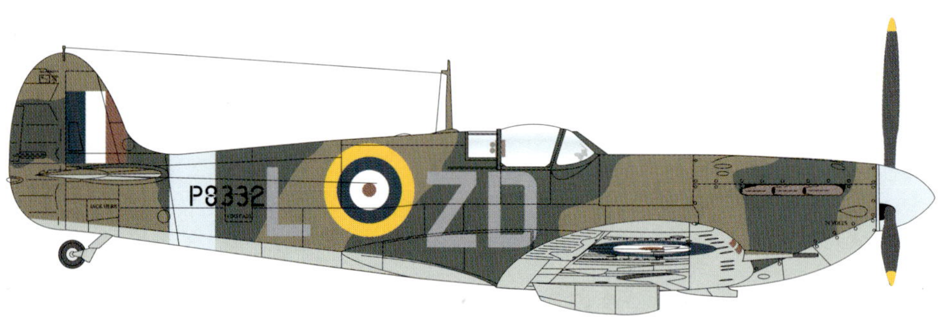

Spitfire Mk IIb, P8332, ZD•L of No 222 (Natal) Squadron, Acklington, July 1941
P8332 was one of some 200 airframes, converted on the production line, from Mk I/II in to the 20mm cannon armed Mk IIb sub-type. P8332 is illustrated still finished in Dark Earth and Dark Green upper surfaces, (in the A Scheme), with Sky under surfaces, a few weeks prior to the change-over to the 'grey and green' Day Fighter Scheme. 56 inch diameter Red/Blue roundels were carried above the wings with 35 inch diameter, Red/White/Blue/Yellow fuselage roundels and 50 inch diameter Red/White/Blue underwing roundels. The Red/White/Blue fin markings were 24 inches wide and 27 inches high. Squadron code letters were approximately 27 inches high in Medium Sea Grey. The 18 inch wide rear fuselage band and the de Havilland propeller spinner were in Sky Blue. The 8 inch high Night serial number was in the usual place on the rear fuselage and had been re-applied over the Sky Blue band where appropriate.

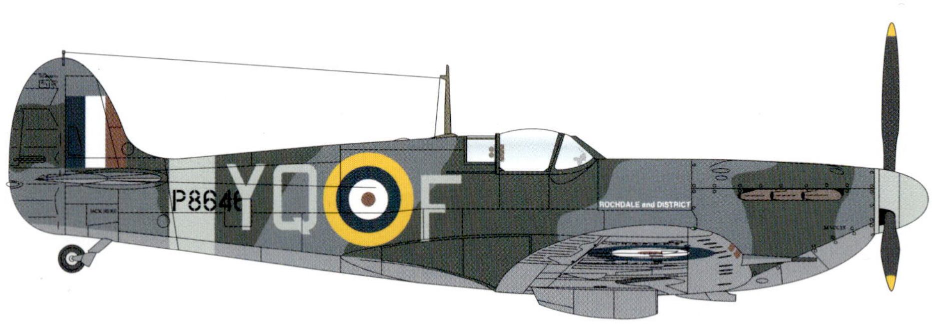

Spitfire Mk IIb, P8646, YQ•F of No 616 (South Yorkshire) Squadron, Kirton-in-Lindsey, October 1941, flown by P/O Alan Hodgkinson
No 616 left its Spitfire Mk Vbs at Tangmere and took over No 65 Squadron's Mk IIbs when it was sent north 'to rest' in October 1941. The upper surfaces of P8646 were Mixed Grey and Dark Green, (in the A Scheme), with Medium Sea Grey under surfaces. Note the lack of Yellow wing leading edges. 56 inch diameter Red/Blue roundels were carried above the wings, with 35 inch diameter, Red/White/Blue/Yellow fuselage roundels and 50 inch diameter Red/White/Blue roundels under the wings. The Red/White/Blue fin marking was 24 inches wide and 27 inches high. Code letters, now correctly utilising the YQ Squadron code allocation, were approximately 24 inches high in Sky. The 18 inch wide rear fuselage band and the Rotol propeller spinner were also probably Sky by this time, as illustrated. The 8 inch high Night serial number was in the usual place on the rear fuselage. Note the presentation name 'Rochdale and District' on starboard cowling side.

Spitfire Mk.II (LR)

Spitfire Mk II (LR), P8388, UM•R of No 152 Squadron, Portreath, June/July 1941

Some 100, randomly selected, Mk II airframes were converted with modified wings and fuel lines to take the asymmetric port wing 30 gallon fuel tank for long-range bomber escort operations over the European continent. Several squadrons, including Nos 66, 234 and 501, were variously partially equipped with the Mk II (LR), as well as No 152, with which P8388 served during the spring and summer of 1941. Finished in Dark Earth and Dark Green upper surfaces, (in the A Scheme), P8388 had Sky under surfaces. 56 inch diameter Red/Blue roundels were carried above the wings with 35 inch diameter, Red/White/Blue/Yellow fuselage roundels and 50 inch diameter Red/White/Blue underwing roundels. The Red/White/Blue fin markings were 24 inches wide and 27 inches high. Squadron code letters were approximately 30 inches high in Medium Sea Grey. The 18 inch wide rear fuselage band and the Rotol propeller spinner were probably in Sky Blue as illustrated. The 8 inch high Night serial number was in the usual place on the rear fuselage and had been re-applied over the Sky Blue band where appropriate.

Spitfire Mk.Va

Spitfire Mk Va, W3185, D•B flown by W/Cdr Douglas Bader, Tangmere, August 1941

Douglas Bader's legendary penchant for 'getting-in-close' to his adversaries and his distrust of the 20mm cannon which had suffered an earlier history of malfunctions, presumably prompted him to opt for using one of the ninety or so 0.303 machine gun-armed Spitfire Mk Vas as his personal aircraft. As a Wing Commander, Bader enjoyed the privilege of having his initials (DB) painted on the fuselage sides instead of squadron codes. W3185, in which Bader was 'shot down' on 9 August, was finished in Dark Earth and Dark Green upper surfaces, (in the A Scheme), with Sky under surfaces. 56 inch diameter Red/Blue roundels were carried above the wings with 35 inch diameter, Red/White/Blue/Yellow fuselage roundels and 50 inch diameter Red/White/Blue underwing roundels. The Red/White/Blue fin markings were 24 inches wide and 27 inches high. W/Cdr Bader's initials were approximately 27 inches high in Medium Sea Grey. The 18 inch wide rear fuselage band and the de Havilland propeller spinner were probably in Sky Blue as illustrated. The 8 inch high Night serial number was in the usual place on the rear fuselage and had been re-applied over the Sky Blue band where appropriate. Note the Wing Commander's pennant on both sides of the cowling.

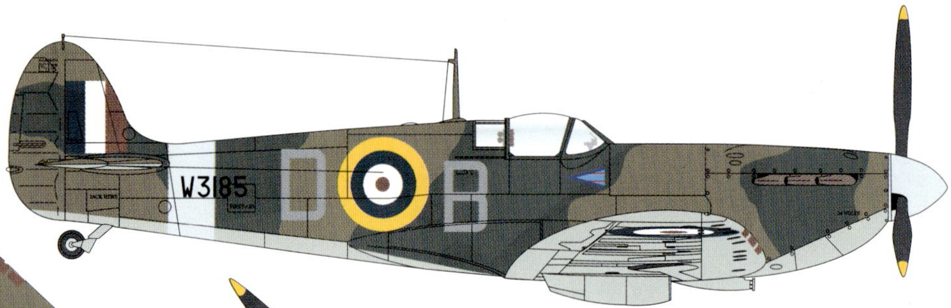

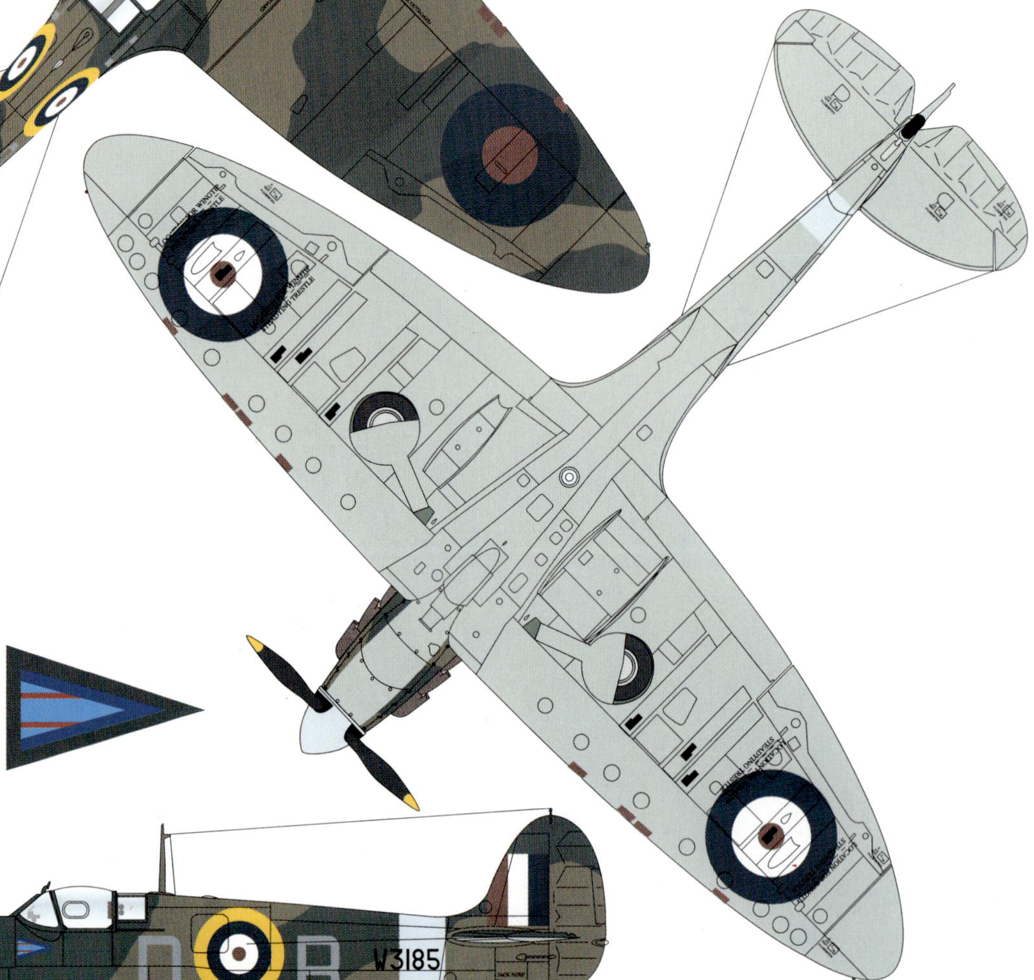

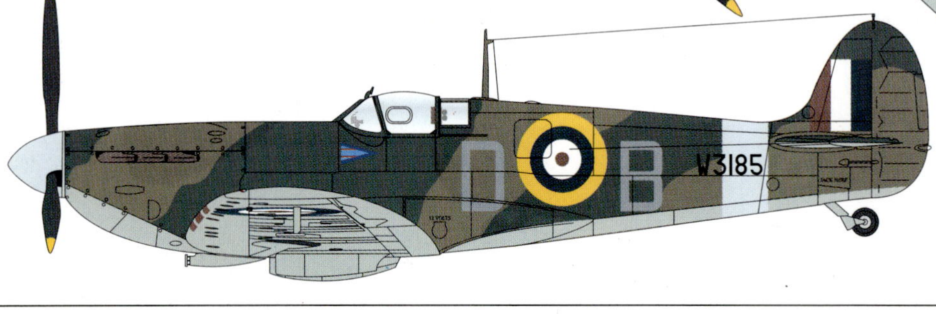

THE AVIATION WORKSHOP LTD
PRODUCT RANGE
(Autumn 2003)

CS-1 SH-60B Seahawk
Upgrade conversion set for Hasegawa kit TBA

CS-2 SH-60B Seahawk TBA

CS-3 SH-60F Oceanhawk TBA

CS-4 HH-60H Seahawk
Conversion set TBA

CS-5 HH-60J Jayhawk
1:72 scale kit with US Coast Guard decals £13.50

CS-6 HH-60H Seahawk - conversion set
Rescuehawk 2000 (HS Squadrons) £8.80

CS-7 S-70B/2 Seahawk - conversion set
RAN version with standard markings £13.50

CS-7S S-70B/2 Seahawk - conversion set
RAN version with tiger tail decals £15.00

CS-8 VH-60N Blackhawk - conversion
US President's aircraft including decals £13.50

CS-9A S-70A/9 Blackhawk
RAAF/Australian Army version with decals £13.50

CS-10 UH-1B/C Huey
RAN conversion with decals £6.00

CS-11 UH-1D/H Huey
RAAF/Australian Army version with decals £7.15

CS-12 UH-1D/H Huey
RAAF/Australian Army version includes resin floats Sold Out

CS-13 US Navy Weapons
General weapons rails for Tomcats, Intruder, A-4 etc TBA

CS-14 T-45C Goshawk
USN improvement set £8.80

CS-15 CH-47C Chinook
RAAF original engine filters and rotor blades (Oz Mods) £7.15

CS-16 Sea King Mk 51A
RAN versions with 90s upgrade (no decals) £8.80

CS-17 SA-365F Daulphin
French Navy conversion and decals TBA

CS-18 HH-3F Pelican
US Coast Guard conversion and decals £13.50

CS-19 AV-8B + Harrier II
Conversion set for Airfix/Heller & Italeri kits £8.80

CS-20 Sea King
Filter box £5.00

CS-21 HH-65A Dolphin
US Coast Guard conversion and decals £5.00

CS-21 S-70B/2 Seahawk
RAN Gulf War conversion and decals £13.50

CS-23 S-2E/G Tracker
RAN conversion and decals £17.50

CS-24 SH-2F Seasprite
RNZN update set and decals sheet £8.80

CS-25 Boeing 707
RAAF version and decals high/low viz schemes £17.50

CS-26 F/A.2 Sea Harrier
Royal Navy conversion set and decals £15.00

CS-27 Hawk 127
RAAF upgrade set and decals for Italeri kit £8.80

CS-28 MB 339CD
RNZAF conversion set and decal sheet £17.50

CS-29 F/A-18 Hornet
Refuelling probe £5.00

CS-30 Blackhawk
HIRSS exhaust kit £5.00

CS-31 MB 326
Improvement set £8.80

CS-32 MB 326
Dropped wing flaps £3.85

CS-33 General
RWR and jammers - mixed set £3.85

CS-34 Hawk T Mk 1A
Red Arrows smoke pod £3.85

CS-35 Sea King
HAS 5/6 radome £3.85

CS-36 SH-27 Seasprite
Fuel tanks £3.85

CS-37 BAe Hawk 127
Dropped wing flaps £3.85

- Coming Soon -

MAK-7201 Aerospatiale AS 350 Squirrel HT Mk 1
Inlcudes RAF and French Armée de Terre decals TBA

MAK-7202 Aerospatiale AS 350 Twin Squirrel
Inlcudes Queen's Flight decals TBA

MAK-7203 Aerospatiale AS 555 Fennec
Incl. Danish Army decals and TPW missile system TBA

MAK-7204 Aerospatiale AS 350B Squirrel
RAN/RAF and DFS including Gulf War modifications TBA

MAK-7205 BAe Sea Harrier F/A.2 TBA

MAK-7206 PC-9 TBA

MAK-7207 MB 326 TBA

MAK-7208 Beech King Air 200 TBA

cont'd on page iv

THE AVIATION WORKSHOP ON TARGET PROFILES

Supermarine Spitfire Mk I - VI in the European Theatre of Operations

Available in 1:72 and 1:48 scales - MA72-114 and MA48-114
see discount order form opposite

1:48 scale example shown same size

To order your

MODEL ALLIANCE

Supermarine Spitfire Mk I - VI
in the European Theatre of Operations
decal sheet

simply fill in the discount coupon at the bottom of the page.
Make sure you indicate whether yo want
1:72 scale (MA72-114)
or
1:48 scale (MA48-114)
and send with your remittance to:-

ON TARGET PROFILES

(DECALS)
The Aviation Workshop Ltd
Brook Barn
Letcombe Regis
Wantage
Oxfordshire OX12 9JD
United Kingdom

Visit our website at www.theaviationworkshop.co.uk

To: **ON TARGET** Decals
The Aviation Workshop
Brook Barn
Letcombe Regis
Wantage
Oxfordshire
OX12 9JD

Name:..

Address:..

....

....

City Post/Zip code:..

Country:..

Please allow 28 days for delivery

Please send me my discount **ON TARGET** Spitfire MkI - VI decals
Please tick decals' scale required:

☐ MA72-114 1/72 scale £6.50 ☐ MA48-114 1/48 scale £8.50

Post free in the UK
Overseas customers please add 20% for P&P

☐ I wish to pay by UK sterling cheque, payable to: *The Aviation Workshop*

☐ I wish to pay by Credit/Debit Card (Please Tick):

Switch Valid From: Issue No.

Card No:

Name on card: ....

Expiry date:

Please enter the last 3 digits on the signature strip:
(reverse side of card):

cont'd from page i

DECALS

MA-100 **Buccaneer**
Gulf War, (all thirteen 'Operation Granby' aircraft)
1:72 £8.80
1:48 £11.00

MA-101 **Buccaneer**
Royal Air Force and Royal Navy aircraft
1:72 £8.80
1:48 £11.00

MA-102 **Harrier GR.7**
Royal Air Force
1:72 £8.80
1:48 £11.00

MA-103 **Westland Sea King**
RN/RAF - HAR.3, HAS.5/6, AEW.2 and HC.4
1:72 £8.80
1:48 £11.00

MA-104 **Tornado GR.1/4**
RAF current squadrons
1:72 £8.80
1:48 £11.00

MA-105 **BAe Hawk T Mk 1**
RAF 1995-2003 - to be released late autumn 2003
1:72 £8.80
1:48 £11.00

MA-106 **RAF Victors -** Release date TBA
1:72 £8.80

MA-107 **BAe Sea Harrier F/A.2**
Royal Navy, all squadrons
1:72 £8.80

MA-108 (MA-601)F-104 Starfighter
1:72 £7.15 - (discount price with book £4.50)
1:48 £8.80 - (discount price with book £6.50)

MA-109 **Operation Telic Pt 1**
RAF - To be released winter 2003
1:72 £8.80 - (discount price with book £6.50)
1:48 £11.00 - (discount price with book £8.50)

MA-110 **Operation Telic Pt 2**
RAF - To be released winter 2003
1:72 £8.80 - (discount price with book £6.50)
1:48 £11.00 - (discount price with book £8.50)

MA-111 **Operation Telic**
Current RAF aircraft stencils - to be released winter 2003
1:72 £8.80 - (discount price with book £6.50)
1:48 £11.00 - (discount price with book £8.50)

MA-112 **Commonwealth Hawks: Pt 1**
1:72 £8.80

MA-113/(MA-602) P-51 Mustang in RAF and Commonwealth service
1:72 £7.15 - (discount price with book £4.50)
1:48 £8.80 - (discount price with book £6.50)

COMING SOON!!

MA-114
Spitfire Mk I to VI: (RAF) European Theatre of Operations
To be released winter 2003
1:72 £8.80 - (discount price with book £6.50)
1:48 £11.00 - (discount price with book £8.50)

MA-115
BAe Hawk in foreign service
To be released winter 2003
1:72 £8.80 - (discount price with book £6.50)
1:48 £11.00 - (discount price with book £8.50)

ON TARGET publications currently available or due for release - as at autumn 2003

ON TARGET PROFILES No 1 **'The Lockheed F-104 Starfighter in worldwide service'** (£9.99) illustrated by Jon Freeman

ON TARGET PROFILES No 2 **'The North American P-51 Mustang in RAF and Commonwealth Air Force service'** (£9.99) illistrated by Jon Freeman

ON TARGET SPECIAL No 1 **'Operation Telic - The colour schemes and markings of the RAF's jets in Operation Iraqi Freedom'**
(£12.99) written by Andy Evans and illustrated by Jon Freeman

ON TARGET PROFILES No 3 **'The British Aerospace Hawk in worldwide service'**
illustrated by Jon Freeman (available November 2003 - £10.99)

ON TARGET SPECIAL No 2 **'Britain Alone - a fascinating selection of colour schemes and markings of British and Commonwealth aircraft operating in the European, Mediterranean and Middle Eastern Theatres of Operations - from June 1940 until December 1941'**
written by Paul Lucas and illustrated by Jon Freeman
(available November 2003 - £TBA)

Order your copies NOW!!

Spitfire Mk.Vb

Spitfire Mk Vb, AB790, J•AK flown by W/Cdr John A Kent, Polish Wing, Northolt, July 1941

A contemporary of Bader's, John Kent was a Canadian national who had joined the RAF in 1935. He began his 'association' with Polish pilots during the Battle of Britain when he was CO of No 303 (Kosciuszko) Squadron and was the first Canadian Wing Leader when he led the Polish Wing, (comprising No 303, 308 and 315 (Polish) Squadrons), from June to August 1941. As a Wing Commander, Kent also enjoyed the privilege of having his initials, (JAK), painted on the fuselage sides of his aircraft instead of squadron codes. AB790 was finished in Dark Earth and Dark Green upper surfaces, (in the A Scheme), with Sky under surfaces. 56 inch diameter Red/Blue roundels were carried above the wings with 35 inch diameter, Red/White/Blue/Yellow fuselage roundels and 50 inch diameter Red/White/Blue underwing roundels. The Red/White/Blue fin markings were 24 inches wide and 27 inches high. W/Cdr Kent's initials were approximately 24 inches high in Medium Sea Grey. The 18 inch wide rear fuselage band and the de Havilland propeller spinner were probably in Sky Blue as illustrated. The 8 inch high Night serial number was in the usual place on the rear fuselage and had been re-applied over the Sky Blue band where appropriate. Note the Wing Commander's pennant, on both sides of the cowling, the Canadian Maple leaf with white Polish Eagle and the words 'John' and 'Thomas' on the respective outer faces of the port and starboard cannon barrel fairings.

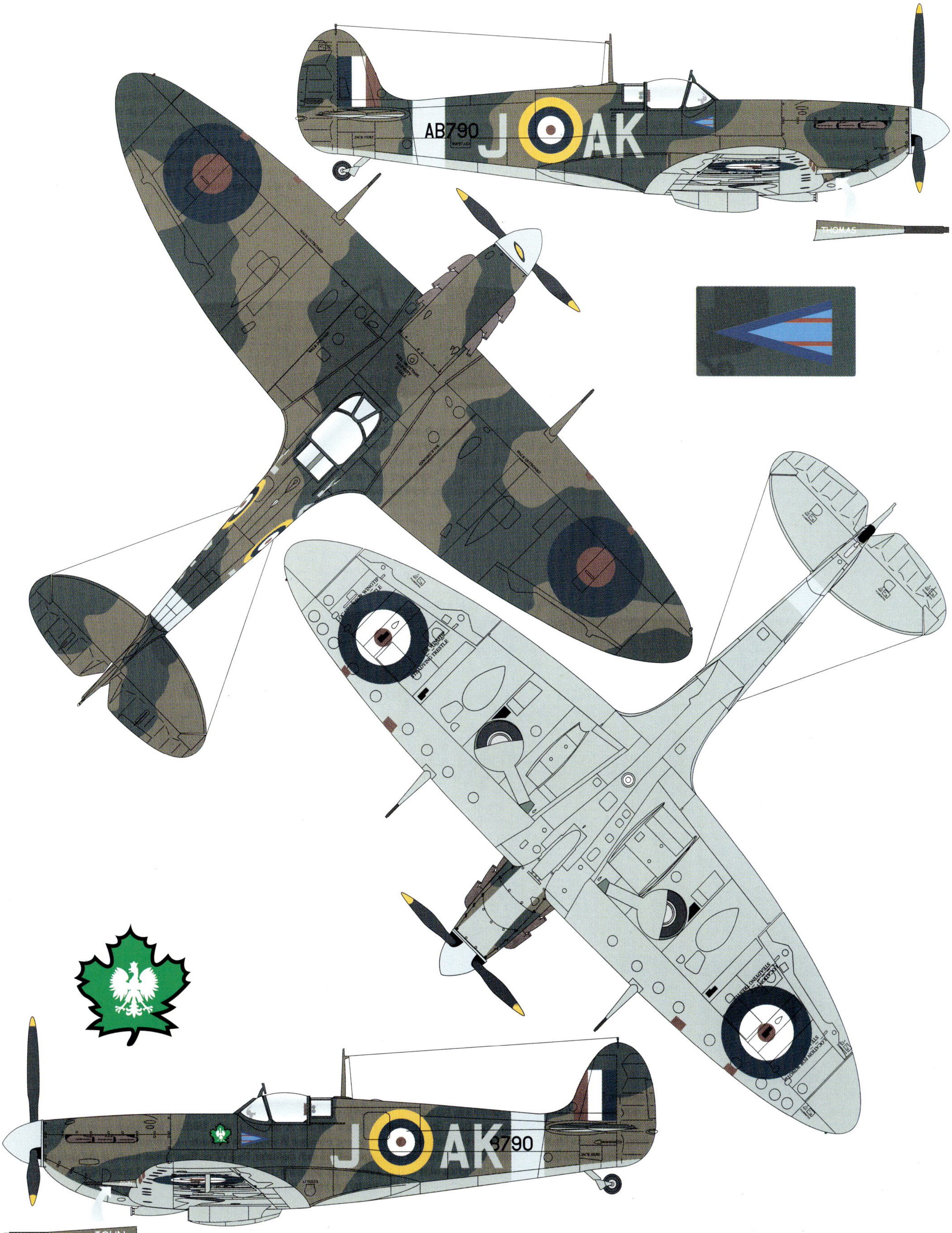

Spitfire Mk.Vb

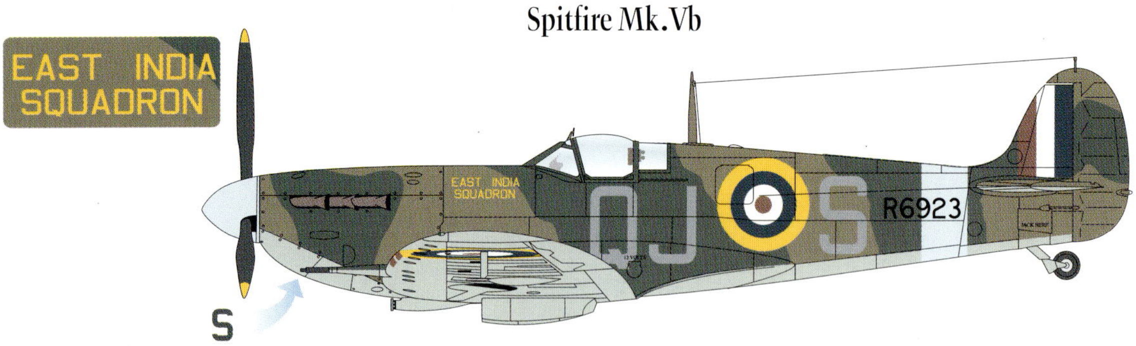

Spitfire Mk Vb, R6923, QJ•S of No 92 Squadron, flown by S/Ldr Jimmy Rankin, Biggin Hill, May/June 1941
R6923 was one of the original cannon-armed Mk Is and had briefly served with No 19 Sqn in July/August 1940. She was subsequently fitted with a Merlin 45 engine and brought up to full Mk Vb standard and issued to No 92 Sqn in April 1941. R6923 was finished in Dark Earth and Dark Green upper surfaces, (in the B Scheme), with Sky under surfaces. 56 inch diameter Red/Blue roundels were carried above the wings with 35 inch diameter, Red/White/Blue/Yellow fuselage roundels and 50 inch diameter Red/White/Blue underwing roundels – the one under the port wing still outlined in Yellow from the period of the Special Night distemper introduced in November 1940 and later removed in mid-April 1941 when the under surfaces of RAF Fighter Command aircraft returned to overall Sky. The Red/White/Blue fin markings were approximately 7 inches wide each and extended the full height of the fin – not yet having been modified to the official 27 inch height. Squadron code letters were approximately 27 inches high in Medium Sea Grey. The 18 inch wide rear fuselage band and the de Havilland propeller spinner may have been in Sky Blue. The 8 inch high Night serial number was in the usual place on the rear fuselage and had been re-applied over the Sky Blue band where appropriate.

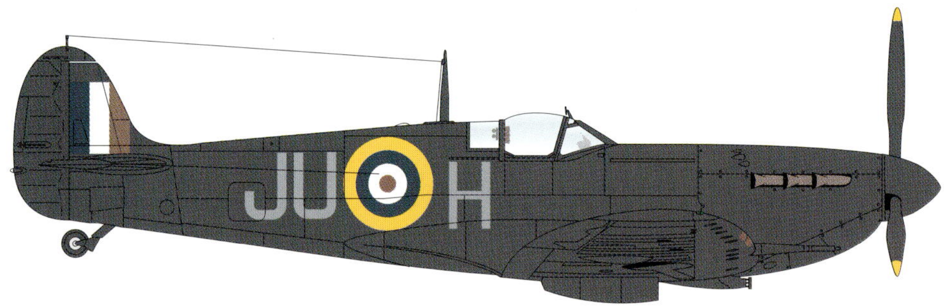

Spitfire Mk Vb, (serial overpainted), JU•H of No 111 Squadron, flown by F/Sgt Peter Durnford, Debden, December 1941
In late December 1941, No 111 Sqn., (together with No 65 Sqn), were ordered to operate in the Night Fighter role following concern that the *Luftwaffe* might resume large scale night attacks on Britain. Accordingly, the squadron's aircraft were re-painted overall in Special Night, obscuring the roundels above and below the wings and just leaving the 35 inch diameter, Red/White/Blue/Yellow roundels on the fuselage and the Red/White/Blue fin markings which were 24 inches wide and 27 inches high. Squadron code letters were retained and were approximately 27 inches high in Medium Sea Grey. The serial number was also overpainted in Special Night as was the de Havilland propeller spinner. Note the 'fish-tail' exhausts and the anti-glare shield on the cowling.

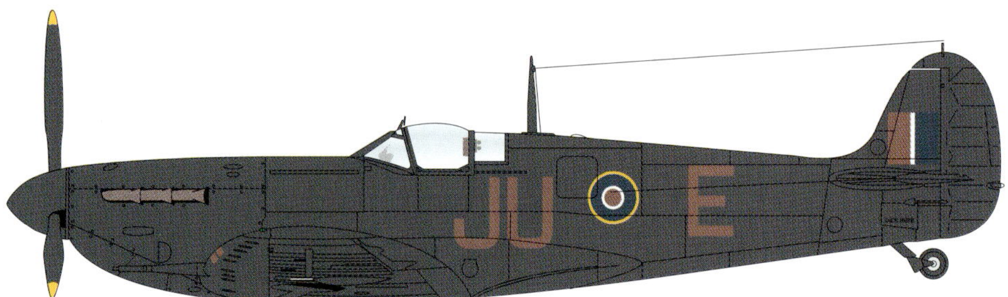

Spitfire Mk Vb, (serial overpainted), JU•E of No 111 Squadron, flown by the CO, S/Ldr Brotchie, Debden, February 1942
JU•E was another of No 111 Squadron's aircraft that was re-painted in overall Special Night, again obscuring the roundels above and below the wings. The standard 35 inch diameter fuselage roundel and the 24 x 27 inch fin flash had also been overpainted and replaced with new 'low-visibility' markings, initially introduced in January 1942 specifically for Night Fighters, comprising 18 inch diameter roundels with reduced White and Yellow areas and 18 inch square fin flashes with a narrow White stripe. These 'low-visibility' markings were adapted and subsequently adopted for all RAF aircraft from mid-May 1942. Squadron code letters were repainted in Red and were approximately 27 inches high. The serial number was overpainted in Special Night as was the de Havilland propeller spinner. Again note the 'fish-tail' exhausts and the anti-glare shield on the cowling.

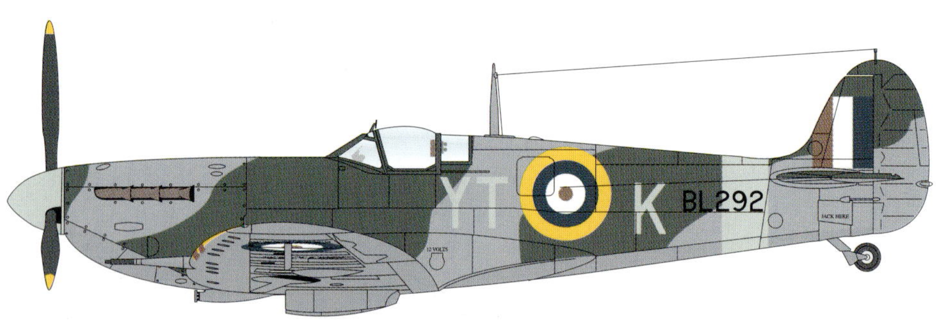

Spitfire Mk Vb, BL292, YT•K of No 65 (East India) Squadron, Debden, March 1942, flown by F/Sgt V Kopecek
The other squadron involved with the Spitfire's short-lived, high speed night interception operations, No 65, also returned to daylight fighter sweeps and bomber escorts in the spring of 1942 and reverted back to the Day Fighter Scheme. BL292 is illustrated with Mixed Grey and Dark Green upper surfaces, (in the A Scheme), with Medium Sea Grey under surfaces. As mentioned previously, Mixed Grey was produced by mixing seven parts Medium Sea Grey to one part Night and could *and did* result in variations in shade – the photograph of BL292 upon which this illustration is based showing a 'light' shade. 56 inch diameter Red/Blue roundels were carried above the wings, with 35 inch diameter, Red/White/Blue/Yellow fuselage roundels and 50 inch diameter Red/White/Blue underwing roundels. The Red/White/Blue fin marking was 24 inches wide and 27 inches high. Squadron codes were approximately 20 inches high – in Sky. The 18 inch wide rear fuselage band and the de Havilland propeller spinner would almost certainly have been in Sky too by this time, with the 8 inch high Night serial number in the usual place on the rear fuselage, applied over the Sky band where appropriate.

Spitfire Mk.Vb

Spitfire Mk Vb, W3458, YQ•X, of No 616 (South Yorkshire) Squadron, August 1941, flown by F/Lt Les 'Buck' Casson

Les Casson was shot down by Adolph Galland on 9 August 1941 – (in the same engagement in which Douglas Bader was 'lost') – in W3458, which was finished in Dark Earth and Dark Green upper surfaces, (in the A Scheme), with Sky under surfaces; the 'grey/green' Day Fighter scheme not being introduced until some days later in mid-August. 56 inch diameter Red/Blue roundels were carried above the wings with 35 inch diameter, Red/White/Blue/Yellow fuselage roundels and 50 inch diameter Red/White/Blue underwing roundels. The Red/White/Blue fin markings were 24 inches wide and 27 inches high. Squadron code letters were approximately 27 inches high in Medium Sea Grey. It was during the summer of 1941, that No 616 Squadron's code letters were changed from QJ to the correct YQ allocation. The 18 inch wide rear fuselage band and the de Havilland propeller spinner were also probably now correctly painted in Sky as illustrated. The 8 inch high Night serial number was in the usual place on the rear fuselage.

Spitfire Mk.Vb

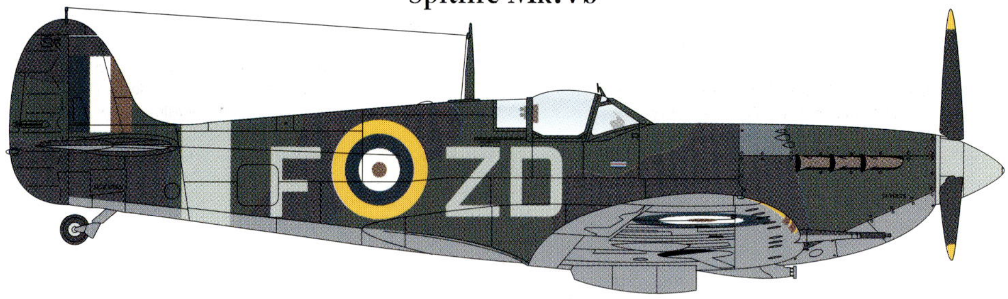

Spitfire Mk Vb, AD233, ZD•F of No 222 (Natal) Squadron, North Weald, April 1942, flown by S/Ldr R M Milne
Initially sporting the presentation name 'West Borneo I' on its cowling, AD233 was originally delivered fresh off the Castle Bromich production line, in September 1941, in the Dark Earth/Dark Green Temperate Land Scheme upper surfaces and Sky undersides. Following re-painting at No 37 MU and several on-squadron 'touch-ups', (where it appears to have lost the presentation name 'West Borneo I' in the process), it is illustrated here as she looked in the late spring of 1942, with Mixed Grey and Dark Green upper surfaces, (in the A Scheme – albeit in a variety of shades!), and Medium Sea Grey under surfaces. 56 inch diameter Red/Blue roundels were carried above the wings, with 35 inch diameter, Red/White/Blue/Yellow fuselage roundels and 50 inch diameter Red/White/Blue underwing roundels. The Red/White/Blue fin marking was 24 inches wide and 27 inches high. Squadron codes were approximately 24 inches high in Sky. The 18 inch wide rear fuselage band and the 'pointed' Rotol propeller spinner were in Sky too. The serial number, usually positioned on the rear fuselage in 8 inch high Night characters, appears to have been painted over, but was possibly re-applied in small, 1 to 2 inch high characters, on the top of the fin .

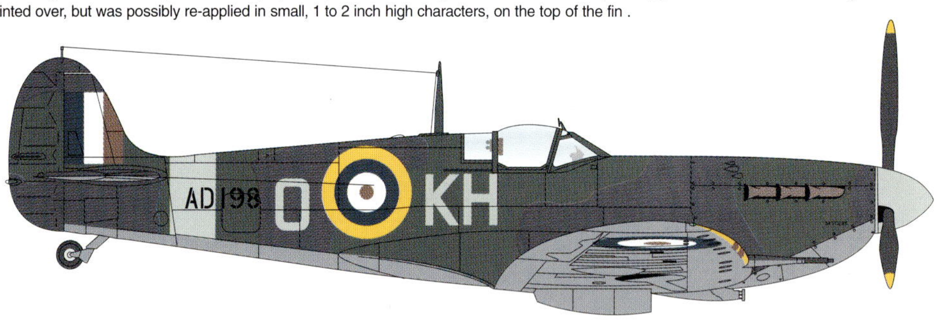

Spitfire Mk Vb, AD198, KH•O of No 403 (Canadian) Squadron, North Weald, April 1942
No 403 was one of some fourteen, Canadian-manned, fighter squadrons that operated during World War Two and AD198 is typical of the hundreds of Spitfires that equipped these squadrons. The upper surfaces are in Mixed Grey and Dark Green, (in the A Scheme), with Medium Sea Grey under surfaces. 56 inch diameter Red/Blue roundels were carried above the wings, with 35 inch diameter, Red/White/Blue/Yellow fuselage roundels and 50 inch diameter Red/White/Blue roundels under the wings. The Red/White/Blue fin marking was 24 inches wide and 27 inches high. Squadron codes were approximately 20 inches high in Sky. The 18 inch wide rear fuselage band and the de Havilland propeller spinner were also in Sky, but note how the rear fuselage band is truncated on the upper/under demarcation line. The 8 inch high Night serial number, (in a stencil style), was in the usual place on the rear fuselage.

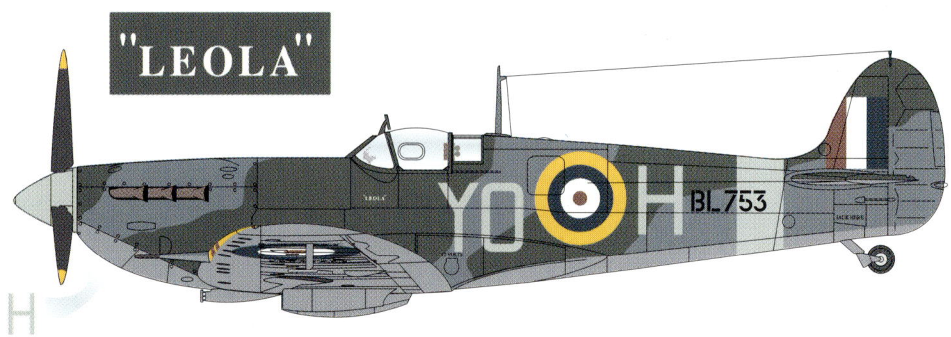

Spitfire Mk Vb, BL753, YO•H of No 401 (Canadian) Squadron, Gravesend, May 1942, flown by P/O Don Blakeslee
No 401 was a pre-war, home-based Canadian unit, originally designated No 1 Sqn RCAF, which moved to the UK in June 1940 and was re-numbered as 401 in March 1941 – presumably to avoid confusion with No 1 Sqn RAF. It received Mk Vbs in October 1941, such as BL753 illustrated here, finished in Mixed Grey and Dark Green upper surfaces, (in the A Scheme), and Medium Sea Grey under surfaces. 56 inch diameter Red/Blue roundels were carried above the wings, with 35 inch diameter, Red/White/Blue/Yellow fuselage roundels and 50 inch diameter Red/White/Blue roundels under the wings. The Red/White/Blue fin marking was 24 inches wide and 27 inches high. Squadron codes were approximately 27 inches high in Sky. The 18 inch wide rear fuselage band and the 'pointed' Rotol propeller spinner were also in Sky. The 8 inch high Night serial number was in the usual place on the rear fuselage. Don Blakeslee was an American national, who joined the RCAF under the Commonwealth Air Training Plan. He transferred to the USAAF later in 1942 and went on to become one of the 4th Fighter Group's most famous 'aces'. Note the personal name *'Leola'*, below the windscreen, in honour of Blakeslee's wife.

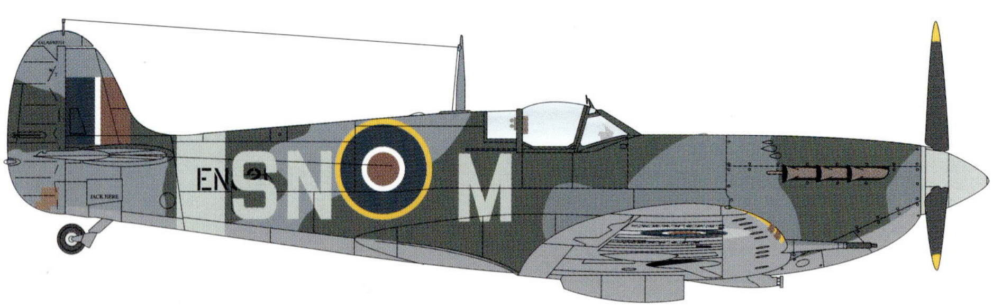

Spitfire Mk Vb, EN821, SN•M of No 243 Squadron, Ouston, July 1942
No 243 re-formed in the UK in June 1942, after losing most of its Brewster Buffalos at Kallang, Singapore, in December 1941, following the Japanese invasion. It was reformed on Spitfire Mk Vbs in June 1942, such as EN821 illustrated here, possibly finished in Ocean Grey and Dark Green upper surfaces, (in the A Scheme), and Medium Sea Grey under surfaces. 56 inch diameter Red/Blue roundels were carried above the wings, but the fuselage and under wing roundels had been modified in to the new style, introduced in mid-May 1942. The Red/White/Blue/Yellow 'National marking III' fuselage roundel was 36 inches in diameter whilst the Red/White/Blue 'National marking II' under wing roundels were 32 inches in diameter. The fin flash, now termed 'Fin marking (i)', was 24 inches wide and 24 inches high. Squadron codes were approximately 24 inches high in Sky. The 18 inch wide rear fuselage band and the 'pointed' Rotol propeller spinner were also in Sky. The 8 inch high Night serial number was in the usual place on the rear fuselage – in a stencil style.

Spitfire Mk.Vb

Spitfire Mk Vb, EP464, NN•E of No 310 (Czech) Squadron, Exeter, early July 1942

No 310 was the first of three fighter squadrons, formed in July 1940, with Czech air and ground personnel who had escaped to the UK. By the spring of 1942, new-build Spitfires on the production line were at last being finished on the production line in the Day Fighter Scheme of Ocean Grey and Dark Green upper surfaces, (in the A Scheme), with Medium Sea Grey under surfaces. 56 inch diameter Red/Blue roundels, (now termed 'National marking I'), were carried above the wings, with the new style, 36 inch diameter Red/White/Blue/Yellow National marking III fuselage roundels and 32 inch diameter Red/White/Blue National marking II under wing roundels. The Fin marking (i), was 24 inches wide and 24 inches high. Squadron codes were approximately 20 inches high in Sky. The 18 inch wide rear fuselage band was in Sky and the 8 inch high Night serial number was in the usual place on the rear fuselage – in a stencil style. The white bands around the cowling and top of the tailplanes and the white 'pointed' Rotol propeller spinner, was a short-lived experiment, within 11 Group at the beginning of July, presumably to assist in the identification of 'friendly' fighters.

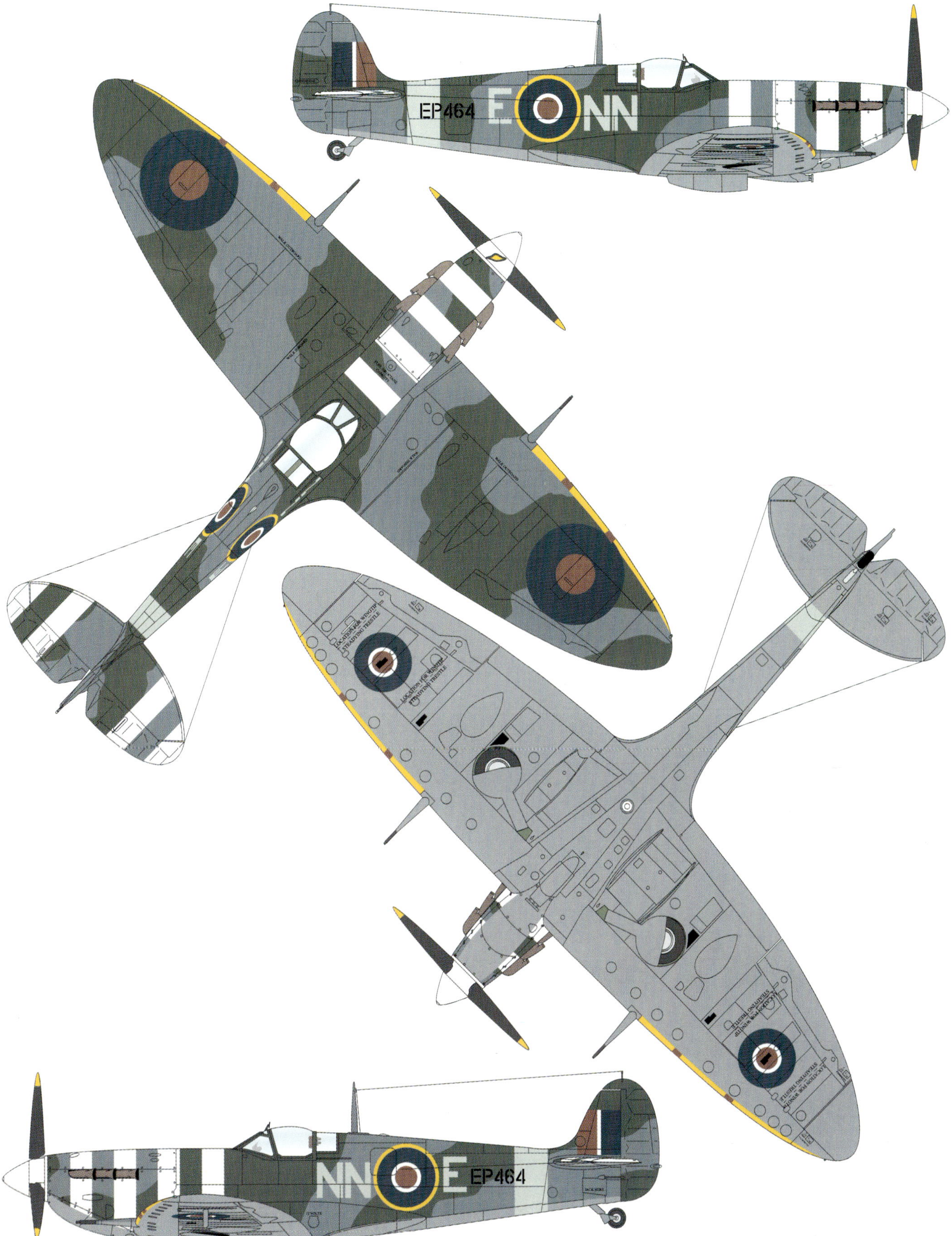

Spitfire Mk.Vb

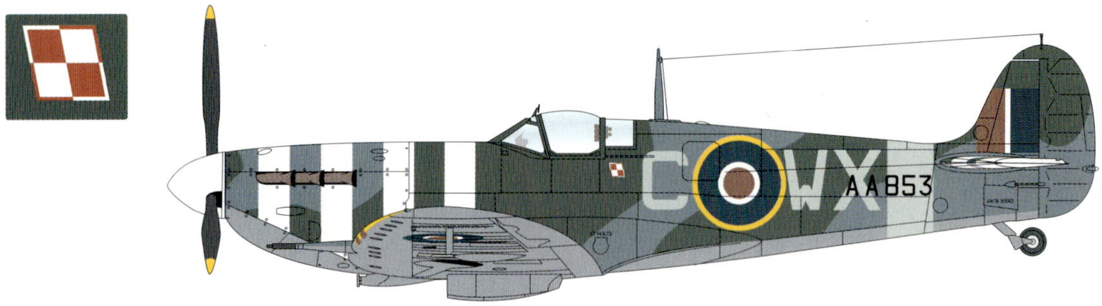

Spitfire Mk Vb, AA853, WX•C of No 302 (Polish) Squadron, Croydon, early July 1942, flown by W/Cdr Stefan Witozenc, 2nd Polish Fighter Wing
No 302 was the first of the Polish-manned fighter squadrons, formed in the UK, and became operational, on Hurricanes, in August 1940. By early 1942, it had been operating Spitfire Mk Vbs for almost nine months, finished in the now standard Day Fighter Scheme of Ocean Grey and Dark Green upper surfaces, (in the A Scheme), and Medium Sea Grey under surfaces. 56 inch diameter Red/Blue National marking I roundels were carried above the wings, with 36 inch diameter Red/White/Blue/Yellow National marking III fuselage roundels and 32 inch diameter Red/White/Blue National marking II under wing roundels. The Fin marking (i), was 24 inches wide and 24 inches high. Squadron codes were carried, despite Witozenc, as a Wing Commander, being eligible to use his own initials, approximately 20 inches high in Sky. The 18 inch wide rear fuselage band was in Sky and the 8 inch high Night serial number was in the usual place on the rear fuselage. The photographs used for the basis of this illustration show AA853 sporting the white bands around the cowling and top of the tailplanes with the de Havilland propeller spinner painted white too, dating the photo to the beginning of July 1942.

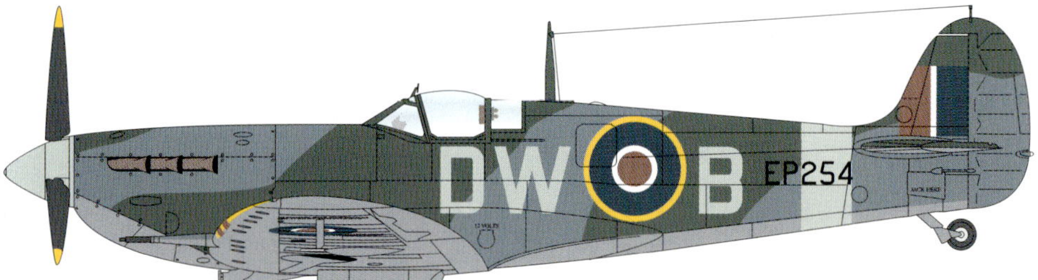

Spitfire Mk Vb, EP254, DW•B of No 610 (County of Chester) Squadron, West Malling, August 1942, flown by S/Ldr J E 'Johnnie' Johnson
No 610 Sqn was 'Johnnie' Johnson's first squadron command, and it is believed that he flew EP254 on the ill-fated 'Operation Jubilee' on 19 August 1942, claiming one 'kill' and a share in another. EP254 was finished in the standard Day Fighter Scheme of Ocean Grey and Dark Green upper surfaces, (in the A Scheme), and Medium Sea Grey under surfaces. 56 inch diameter Red/Blue National marking I roundels were carried above the wings, with 36 inch diameter Red/White/Blue/Yellow National marking III fuselage roundels and 32 inch diameter Red/White/Blue National marking II under wing roundels. The Fin marking (i), was 24 inches wide and 24 inches high. Squadron codes were approximately 24 inches high in Sky. The 18 inch wide rear fuselage band and the 'pointed' Rotol propeller spinner were in Sky, with the 8 inch high Night serial number in the usual place on the rear fuselage. The individual aircraft letter may have been applied under the nose – possibly 12 inches high and also in Sky

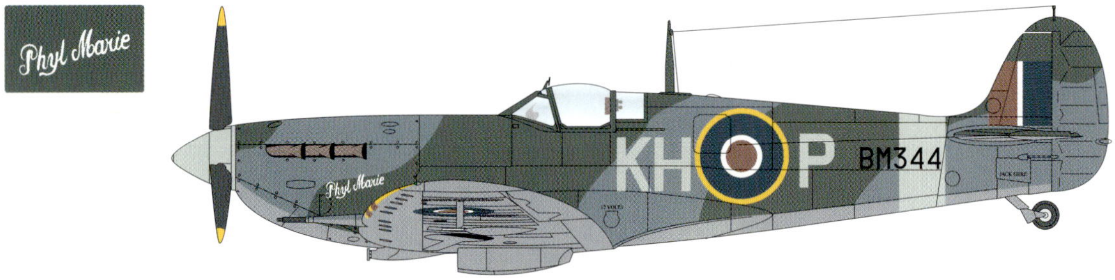

Spitfire Mk Vb, BM344, KH•P of No 403 (Canadian) Squadron, Manston, August 1942, flown by S/Ldr Syd Ford
BM344, also took part in 'Operation Jubilee' on 19 August 1942, flown by S/Ldr Syd Ford the unit's CO, and was finished in the standard Day Fighter Scheme of Ocean Grey and Dark Green upper surfaces, (in the A Scheme), and Medium Sea Grey under surfaces. 56 inch diameter Red/Blue National marking I roundels were carried above the wings, with 36 inch diameter Red/White/Blue/Yellow National marking III fuselage roundels and 32 inch diameter Red/White/Blue National marking II under wing roundels. The Fin marking (i), was 24 inches wide and 24 inches high. Squadron codes were approximately 20 inches high in Sky. The 18 inch wide rear fuselage band and the 'pointed' Rotol propeller spinner were also in Sky, with the 8 inch high Night serial number in the usual place on the rear fuselage. Note S/Ldr Ford's personal name *'Phyl Marie'* on the cowling side.

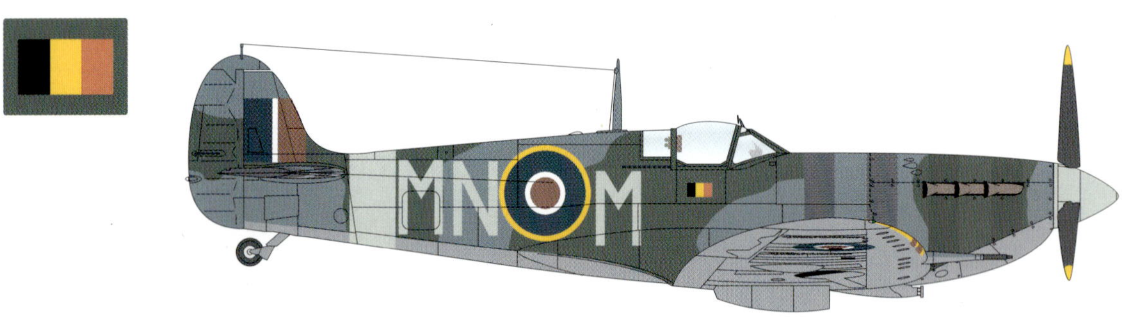

Spitfire Mk Vb, AB967, MN•M of No 350 (Belgian) Squadron, Rochford, September 1942
Still bearing residual evidence of the short-lived experiment within 11 Group at the beginning of July, AB967 is illustrated as she looked a little later in the year, finished in the standard Day Fighter Scheme of Ocean Grey and Dark Green upper surfaces, (in the A Scheme), with Medium Sea Grey under surfaces. 56 inch diameter Red/Blue National marking I roundels were carried above the wings, with 36 inch diameter Red/White/Blue/Yellow National marking III fuselage roundels and 32 inch diameter Red/White/Blue National marking II under wing roundels. The Fin marking (i), was 24 inches wide and 24 inches high. Squadron codes were approximately 27 inches high in Sky. The 18 inch wide rear fuselage band and the 'pointed' Rotol propeller spinner were also in Sky. The serial number appears to have been painted out but may have been re-applied in small characters at the top of the fin. Note also the 'painted-out' (?) bands around the cowling and the Belgian tri-colour flag under the canopy hood.

Spitfire Mk.Vb

Spitfire Mk Vb, EN951, RF•D of No 303 (Kosciusko) Squadron, Kirton-in-Lindsey, September 1942, flown by S/Ldr Jan Zumbach

'Johann' Zumbach flew several Spitfires that carried his famous 'Donald Duck' personal emblem, but we have chosen to illustrate the last one he flew as CO of No 303, which incidentally sported the largest rendition of 'Donald Duck' of them all! EN951 was finished in the standard Day Fighter Scheme of Ocean Grey and Dark Green upper surfaces, (in the A Scheme pattern), with Medium Sea Grey under surfaces. 56 inch diameter Red/Blue National marking I roundels were carried above the wings, with 36 inch diameter Red/White/Blue/Yellow National marking III fuselage roundels and 32 inch diameter Red/White/Blue National marking II under wing roundels. The Fin marking (i), was 24 inches wide and 24 inches high. Squadron codes were approximately 20 inches high in Sky, with the individual aircraft letter repeated under the nose in Sky. The 18 inch wide rear fuselage band and the 'pointed' Rotol propeller spinner were also in Sky. The serial number appears to have been re-applied in smaller, 2-3 inch high characters, much higher on the rear fuselage band. Note the Polish flag on both sides of the nose; the *Kosciusko* Squadron badge under the windscreen, again on both sides; the Squadron Leader rank pennant under the windscreen on the port side only; the scoreboard on the port side showing fourteen white outlined crosses, the last one with a '1/3' in it referring to the thirteen and one third Confirmed 'kills' claimed by Zumbach up to August 1942, plus four red outlined crosses referring to his claimed Probables; the 'egg laying' (?) Donald Duck cartoon, on the port side only; and finally the tall rear view mirror.

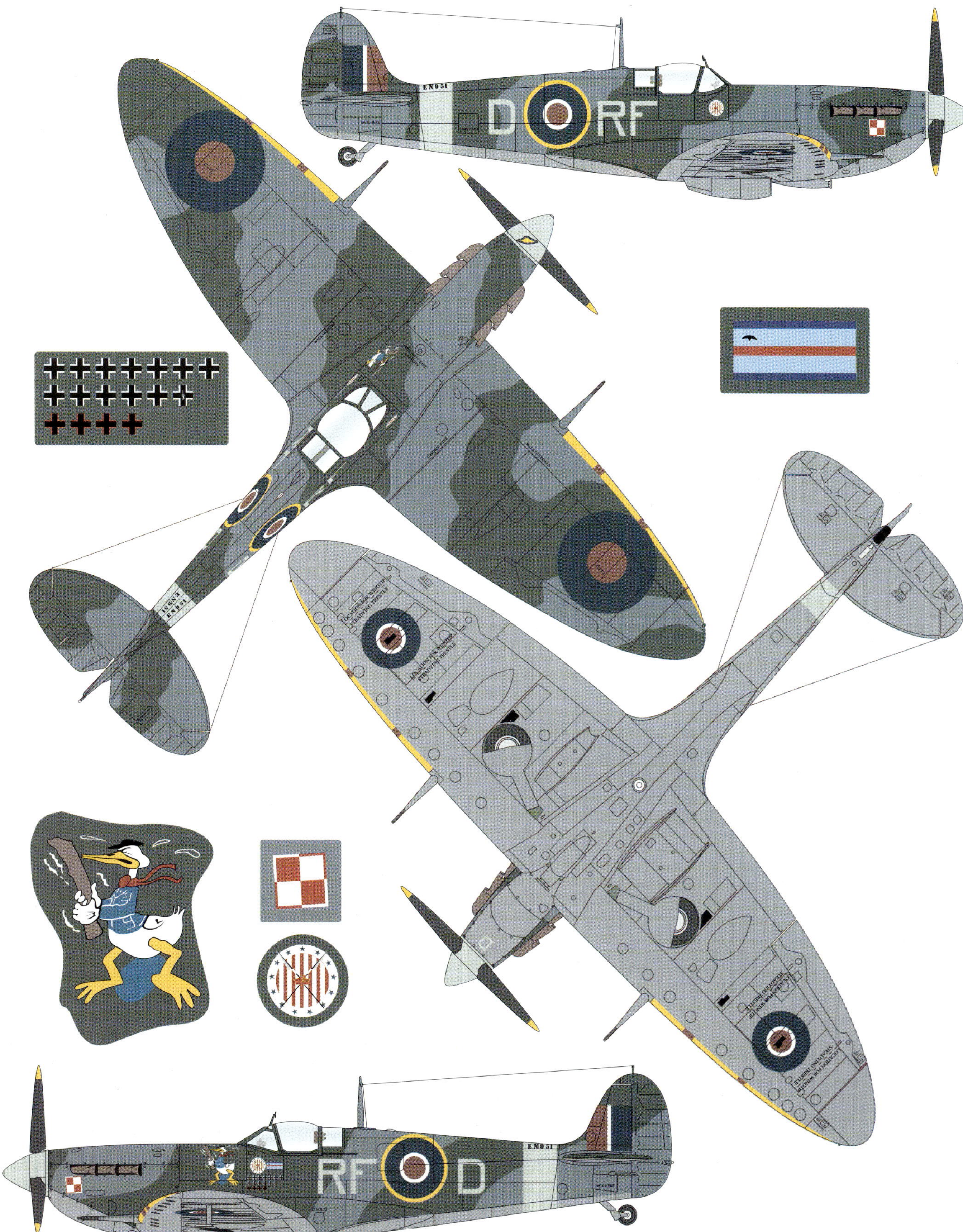

Spitfire Mk.Vb

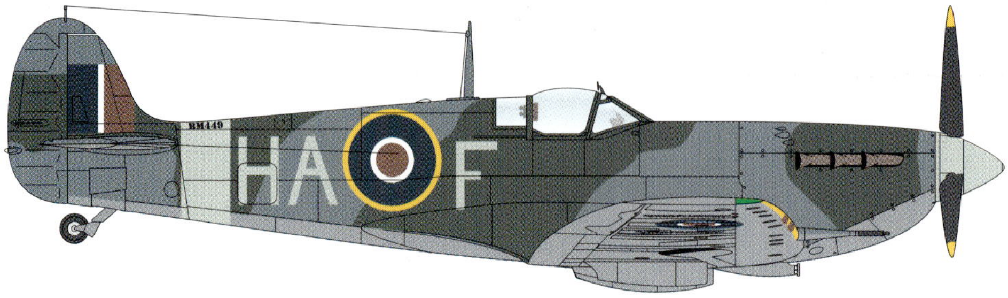

Spitfire Mk Vb, BM449, AF•H of the Air Fighting Development Unit (AFDU), Duxford, early 1943
One of the few 'non-combatant' aircraft in this book, we have chosen BM449 to illustrate that sometimes things are not always what they seem! The placing of the code letters on the fuselage would indicate that the aircraft belonged to No 218 Sqn., (a bomber unit that never operated Spitfires), when in fact the codes should read AF•H and have only been wrongly positioned on (both sides of) the fuselage. Other than this interesting anomaly, BM449 was finished in the standard Day Fighter Scheme of Ocean Grey and Dark Green upper surfaces, (in the A Scheme), and Medium Sea Grey under surfaces. 56 inch diameter Red/Blue National marking I roundels were carried above the wings, with 36 inch diameter Red/White/Blue/Yellow National marking III fuselage roundels and 32 inch diameter Red/White/Blue National marking II under wing roundels. The Fin marking (i), was 24 inches wide and 24 inches high. The unit codes were approximately 24 inches high in Sky. The 18 inch wide rear fuselage band and the 'pointed' Rotol propeller spinner were also in Sky, with the serial number in smaller, 2-3 inch high characters, much higher on the rear fuselage band. Note this aircraft had 'clipped' wing tips.

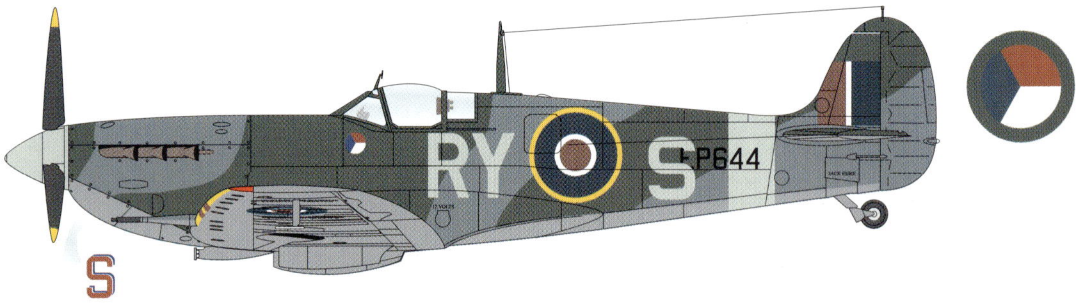

Spitfire Mk Vb, EP644, RY•S of No 313 (Czech) Squadron, Church Stanton, March 1943
No 313 was the third Czech-manned fighter squadron to form in the UK, becaming operational in May 1941. By early 1943, it was operating 'clipped-wing' Spitfire Mk Vbs on offensive operations, finished in the standard Day Fighter Scheme of Ocean Grey and Dark Green upper surfaces, (in the A Scheme), and Medium Sea Grey under surfaces. 56 inch diameter Red/Blue National marking I roundels were carried above the wings, with 36 inch diameter Red/White/Blue/Yellow National marking III fuselage roundels and 32 inch diameter Red/White/Blue National marking II under wing roundels. The Fin marking (i), was 24 inches wide and 24 inches high. Squadron codes were approximately 24 inches high in Sky. The 18 inch wide rear fuselage band and the 'pointed' Rotol propeller were in Sky, and the 8 inch high Night serial number was in the usual place on the rear fuselage. Note the Czech national marking under the windscreen and the 18 inch high Red, with a black 'shadow', individual aircraft letter under the nose.

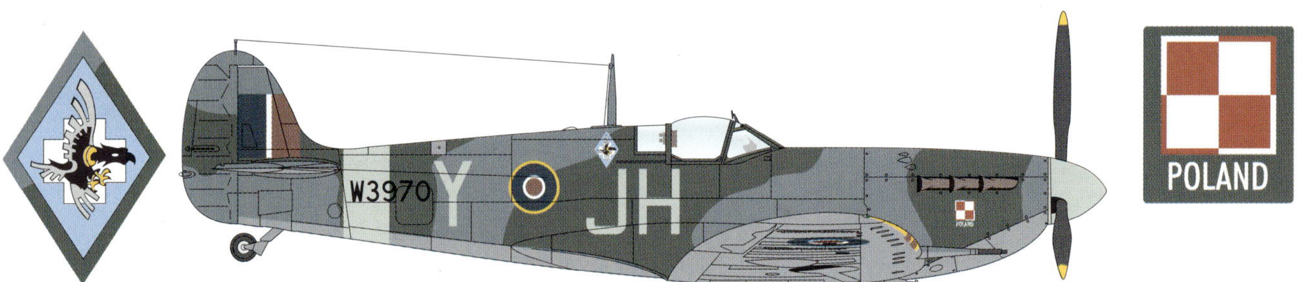

Spitfire Mk Vb, W3970, JH•Y of No 317 (Wilenski) Squadron, Kirton-in-Lindsey, circa spring 1943
Another Polish-manned fighter squadron and another example of marking anomalies, in that W3970 had a 21 inch diameter Red/White/Blue/Yellow National marking III fuselage roundel applied instead of the standard 36 inch diameter style. Other than that, W3970 was finished in the standard Day Fighter Scheme of Ocean Grey and Dark Green upper surfaces, (in the A Scheme), and Medium Sea Grey under surfaces. 56 inch diameter Red/Blue National marking I roundels were carried above the wings, with 32 inch diameter Red/White/Blue National marking II under wing roundels. The Fin marking (i), was 24 inches wide and 24 inches high. Squadron codes were approximately 24 inches high in Sky. The 18 inch wide rear fuselage band and the de Havilland propeller were in Sky, and the 8 inch high Night serial number was in the usual place on the rear fuselage. Note the Polish national marking under the exhaust manifolds and the *Wilenski* badge just behind the cockpit area.

Spitfire Mk Vb, BL767, WN•Z of No 527 (Radar Calibration) Squadron, Digby, circa early 1945
Another 'non-combatant' squadron example, this time illustrating the longevity of some airfarmes. BL767 was first issued to No 54 Sqn in February 1942 and passed through the hands of at least another four operational squadrons until its service with 527 Sqn., after which it was Struck Off Charge on 31 January 1945. Finished in the standard Day Fighter Scheme of Ocean Grey and Dark Green upper surfaces, (in the A Scheme), with Medium Sea Grey under surfaces. 56 inch diameter Red/Blue National marking I roundels were carried above the wings, with 36 inch diameter Red/White/Blue/Yellow National marking III fuselage roundels and 32 inch diameter Red/White/Blue National marking II under wing roundels. The Fin marking (i), was 24 inches wide and 24 inches high. Squadron codes were approximately 20 inches high in Sky, with the 18 inch wide rear fuselage band in Sky. The 'pointed' Rotol propeller spinner was Red, with what appears to be a white backplate. The serial number appears to have been re-applied much further to the rear, to a position under the tailplanes. Note the name *Anna* just infront of the windscreen.

Spitfire Mk.Vb

Spitfire Mk Vb, EN921, YO•A of No 401 (Canadian) Squadron, Biggin Hill, October 1943, flown by F/O Jack Sheppard

EN921 probably sported one of the largest pieces of risqué artwork ever applied to a Spitfire and therefore virtually guarenteed its inclusion in this book! Finished in the standard Day Fighter Scheme of Ocean Grey and Dark Green upper surfaces in a repainted and much modified version of the A Scheme – see the area around the cockpit which appears to have transposed the Dark Green and Ocean Grey colours – with Medium Sea Grey under surfaces. EN921 also operated with 'clipped' wing tips for much of its service with 401 Squadron. 56 inch diameter Red/Blue National marking I roundels were carried above the wings, with 36 inch diameter Red/White/Blue/Yellow National marking III fuselage roundels and 32 inch diameter Red/White/Blue National marking II under wing roundels. The Fin marking (i), was 24 inches wide and 24 inches high. Squadron codes were approximately 27 inches high in Sky, with the individual aircraft letter repeated under the nose in black on a white disc. The 18 inch wide rear fuselage band and the 'pointed' Rotol propeller spinner were also in Sky, and the 8 inch high Night serial number was in the usual place on the rear fuselage. Possibly (!?!) the most striking marking on EN921 is the 'nude' on the port cowling side!

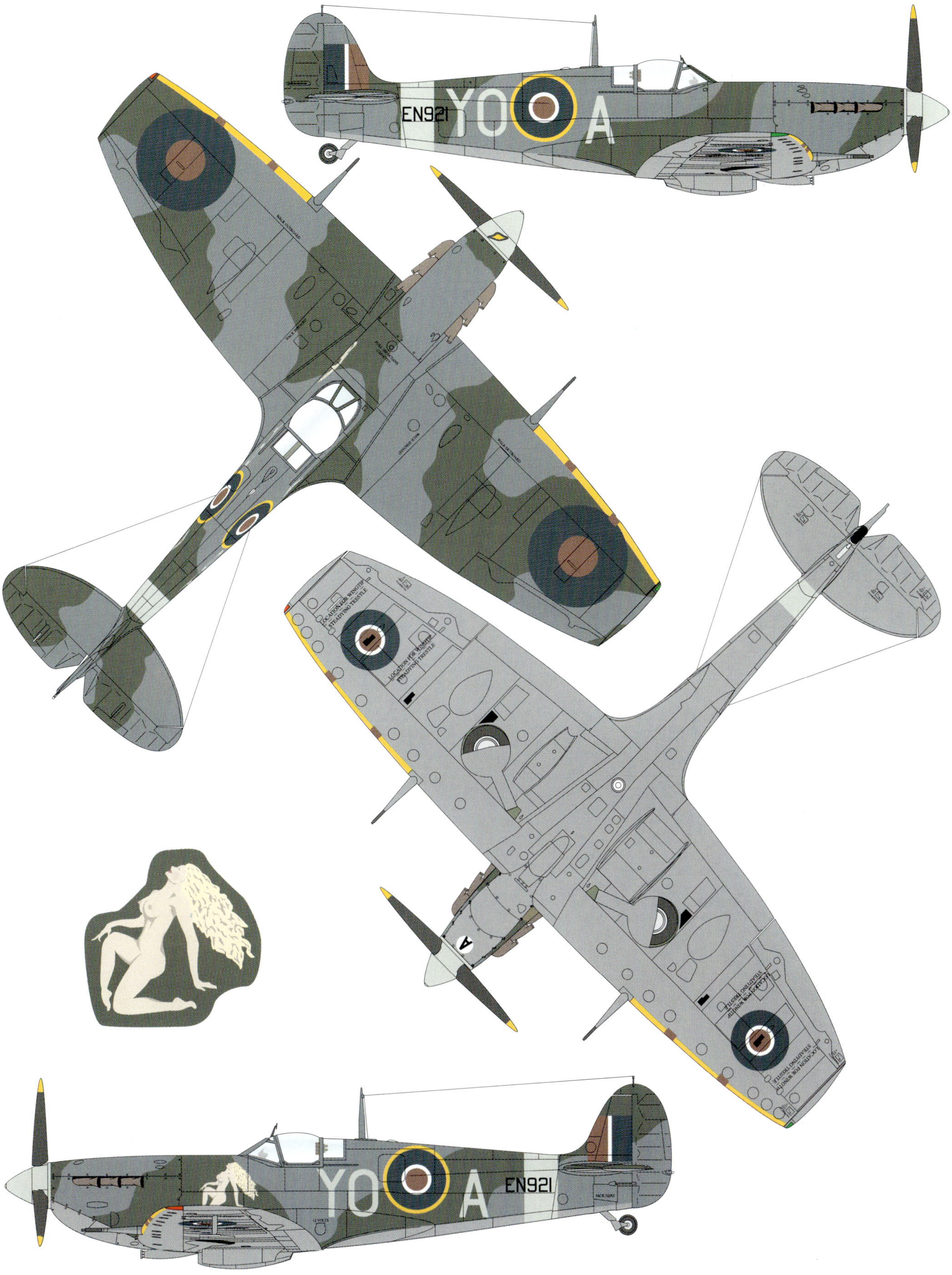

Spitfire Mk.Vb

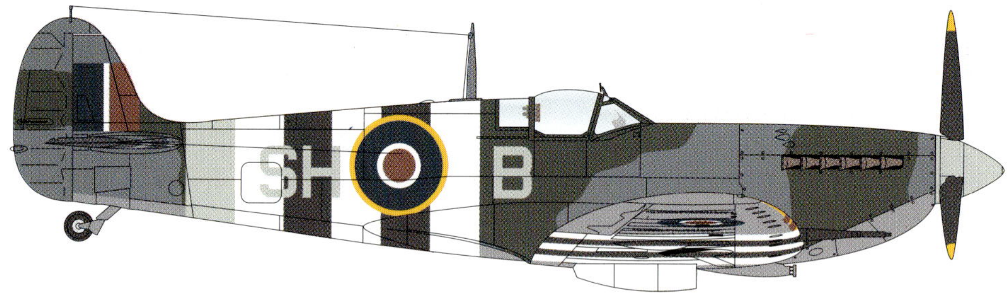

Spitfire Mk Vb, BL734, SH•B of No 64 Squadron, Deanland, early June 1944
Marked up with black and white 'invasion stripes' on the evening of 5 June, BL734 was finished in the standard Day Fighter Scheme of Ocean Grey and Dark Green upper surfaces, (in the A Scheme), with Medium Sea Grey under surfaces. 56 inch diameter Red/Blue National marking I roundels were carried above the wings, with 36 inch diameter Red/White/Blue/Yellow National marking III fuselage roundels and 32 inch diameter Red/White/Blue National marking II under wing roundels. The Fin marking (i), was 24 inches wide and 24 inches high. Squadron codes were approximately 18 inches high in Sky, with the 18 inch wide rear fuselage band and the 'pointed' Rotol propeller spinner also in Sky. The serial number appears to have been painted over but may have been re-applied in smaller characters at the top of the fin. Note the multiple exhaust manifolds – retro-fitted to many of the Mk Vbs still operational in the early summer of 1944

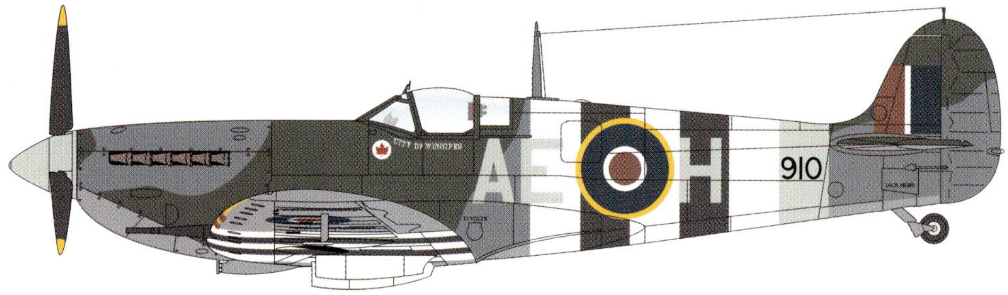

Spitfire Mk Vb, AB910, AE•H of No 402 (Canadian) Squadron, Horne, early June 1944
Marked up with black and white 'invasion stripes', AB910 was finished in the standard Day Fighter Scheme of Ocean Grey and Dark Green upper surfaces, (in the A Scheme), with Medium Sea Grey under surfaces. 56 inch diameter Red/Blue National marking I roundels were carried above the wings, with 36 inch diameter Red/White/Blue/Yellow National marking III fuselage roundels and 32 inch diameter Red/White/Blue National marking II under wing roundels. The Fin marking (i), was 24 inches wide and 24 inches high. Squadron codes were approximately 24 inches high in Sky, with the 18 inch wide rear fuselage band and the 'pointed' Rotol propeller spinner also in Sky. The 8 inch high Night serial number was in the usual position but was partially obscurred by the invasion stripes. Note the red Canadian Maple leaf and the *'City of Winnipeg'* wording under the cockpit and the multiple exhaust manifolds.

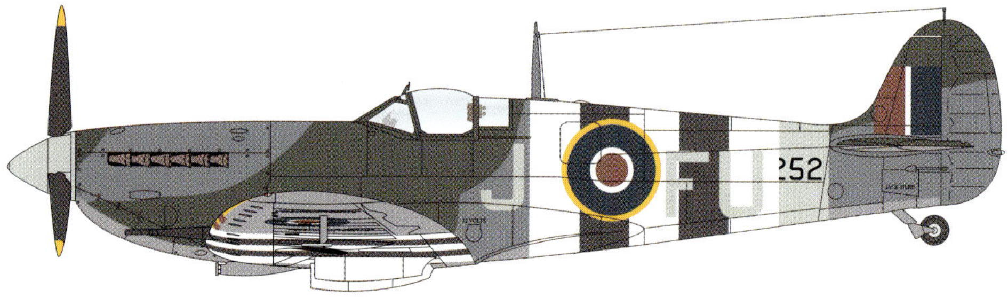

Spitfire Mk Vb, EP252, FU•J of No 453 (Australian) Squadron, Ford, early June 1944
No 453 was one of several fighter squadrons covering the D-Day landings which was still operating a mix of Mk Vs, (both Vbs and Vcs), and Mk IXcs. Marked up with black and white 'invasion stripes', EP252, which had been with the squadron since the end of 1943, was finished in the standard Day Fighter Scheme of Ocean Grey and Dark Green upper surfaces, (in the A Scheme), with Medium Sea Grey under surfaces. 56 inch diameter Red/Blue National marking I roundels were carried above the wings, with 36 inch diameter Red/White/Blue/Yellow National marking III fuselage roundels and 32 inch diameter Red/White/Blue National marking II under wing roundels. The Fin marking (i), was 24 inches wide and 24 inches high. Squadron codes were approximately 24 inches high in Sky, with the 18 inch wide rear fuselage band and the 'pointed' Rotol propeller spinner also in Sky. The 8 inch high Night serial number was in the usual position but was partially obscured by the invasion stripes. Note the multiple exhaust manifolds.

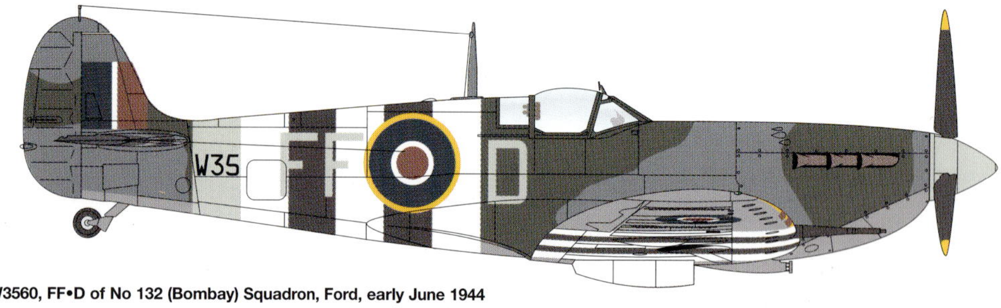

Spitfire Mk Vb, W3560, FF•D of No 132 (Bombay) Squadron, Ford, early June 1944
No 132 was another fighter squadron operating a mix of Mk Vs and Mk IXcs in June/July 1944. Marked up with black and white 'invasion stripes', W3560, another long-serving airframe, was finished in the standard Day Fighter Scheme of Ocean Grey and Dark Green upper surfaces, (in the A Scheme), with Medium Sea Grey under surfaces. 56 inch diameter Red/Blue National marking I roundels were carried above the wings, with 36 inch diameter Red/White/Blue/Yellow National marking III fuselage roundels and 32 inch diameter Red/White/Blue National marking II under wing roundels. The Fin marking (i), was 24 inches wide and 24 inches high. Squadron codes were approximately 24 inches high in Sky, with the 18 inch wide rear fuselage band and the 'pointed' Rotol propeller spinner also in Sky. The 8 inch high Night serial number was in the usual position but was partially obscured by the invasion stripes. Note that W3560 had not yet been updated with multiple exhaust manifolds.

Spitfire Mk.Vb

Spitfire Mk Vb, BL415, AZ•B of No 234 (Madras) Squadron, Deanland, early June 1944, flown by F/Lt Walt 'Johnny' Johnston

BL415 can be regarded as 'typical' of the many Spitfire Mk Vbs that were still equipping front-line fighter squadrons in the early summer of 1944. Referred to by the pilots and ground crews as 'Clipped, Cropped and Clapped' – relating to the *'clipped'* wing tips which improved the rate of roll below 10,000ft; *'cropped'* engine supercharger blower which improved power, again below 10,000ft; and *'clapped-out'* airframes, most of them having previously seen intensive operational service with several squadrons already. Many, such as BL415 illustrated here, had been progressively updated throughout their service lives, with ongoing improvements that had been introduced on newer Marks, such as six-stack multiple exhaust manifolds and enlarged horn balance elevators. The order to apply the Allied Expeditionary Air Force 'invasion stripes', (or 'Distinctive Marking - Aircraft' as the SHAEF Operational Memorandum No 23 refers to them!), requiring single-engined fighters to have 18 inch wide bands – two black and three white – around the circumference of the fuselage, 18 inches infront of the tailplanes, and around both surfaces of the mainplanes, was given on the evening of 4 June, but due to the invasion being temporarily cancelled, those aircraft not yet marked up were left until the evening of 5 June – at which time BL415 was also undergoing a complete engine change!

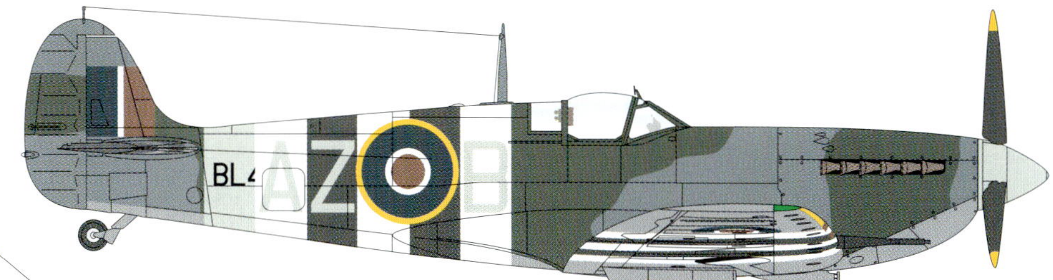

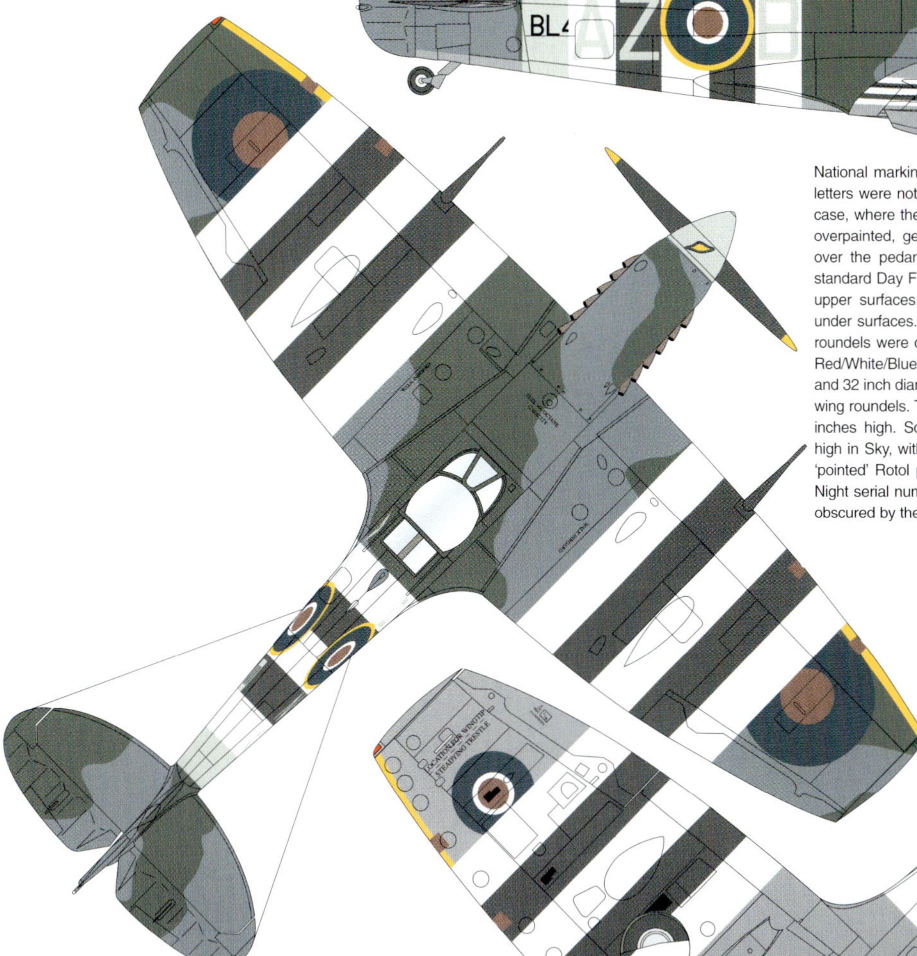

National markings, serial numbers and squadron identification letters were not supposed to be obstructed, but as in BL415's case, where the upper and under wing roundels were partially overpainted, getting the invasion stripes applied took priority over the pedantics of the order. BL415 was finished in the standard Day Fighter Scheme of Ocean Grey and Dark Green upper surfaces, (in the A Scheme), with Medium Sea Grey under surfaces. 56 inch diameter Red/Blue National marking I roundels were carried above the wings, with 36 inch diameter Red/White/Blue/Yellow National marking III fuselage roundels and 32 inch diameter Red/White/Blue National marking II under wing roundels. The Fin marking (i), was 24 inches wide and 24 inches high. Squadron codes were approximately 24 inches high in Sky, with the 18 inch wide rear fuselage band and the 'pointed' Rotol propeller spinner also in Sky. The 8 inch high Night serial number was in the usual position but was partially obscured by the invasion stripes.

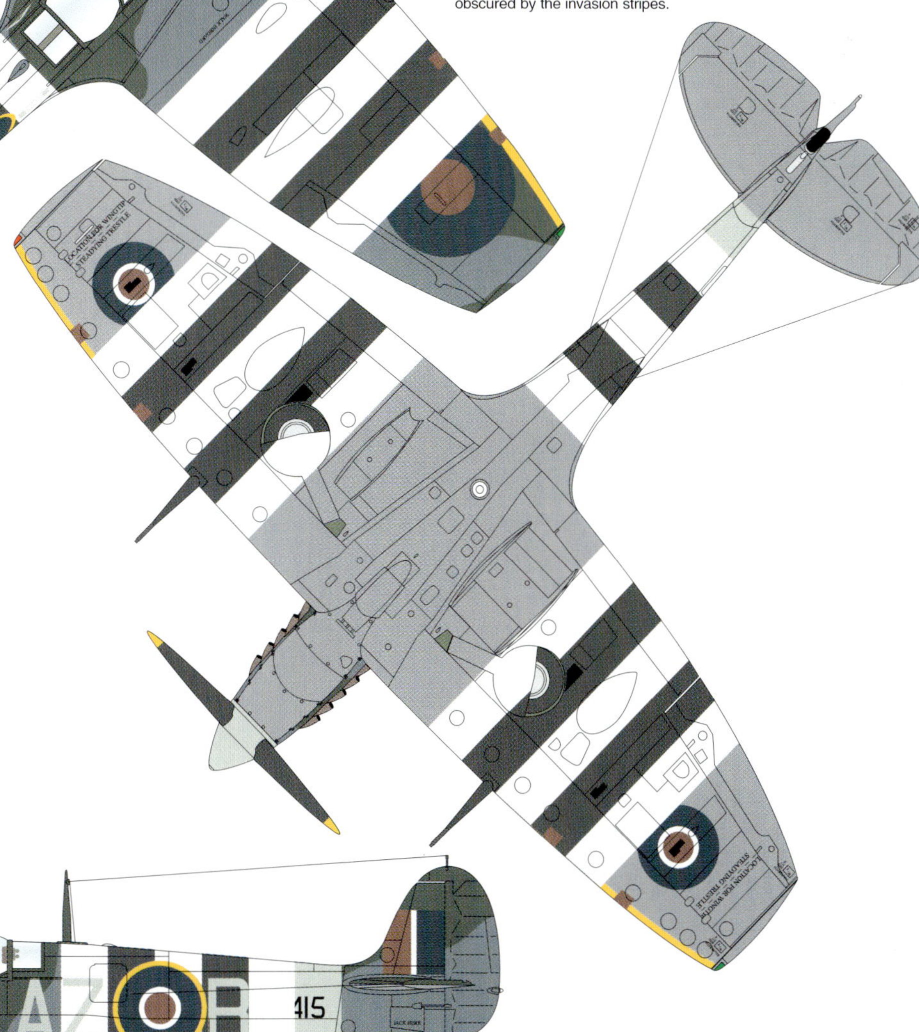

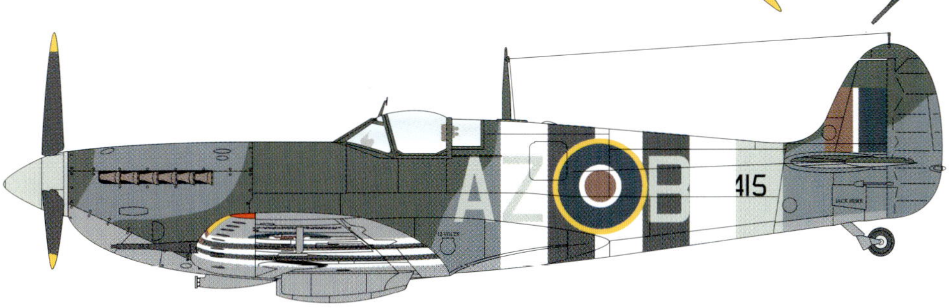

Spitfire Mk.Vc

Spitfire Mk Vc, AB216, DL•Z of No 91 (Nigeria) Squadron, Hawkinge, May 1942, flown by S/Ldr Robert 'Bobby' Oxspring
The Mk Vc was a development of the Mk Vb, fitted with the so-called 'universal wing', which was able to be fitted with the 'c' armament of two 20mm cannon and two 0.303 inch machine guns, and associated ammunition, per wing. Operationally, very few Mk Vcs were actually fitted with the four cannon option, standardising on one 20mm cannon per wing with the outer bay capped with a small domed fairing. AB216 was an early production machine taken on No 91 Squadron's charge in January 1942, and as such was finished in Mixed Grey and Dark Green upper surfaces, (in the A Scheme), with Medium Sea Grey under surfaces. 56 inch diameter Red/Blue roundels were carried above the wings, with 35 inch diameter, Red/White/Blue/Yellow fuselage roundels and 50 inch diameter Red/White/Blue roundels under the wings. The Red/White/Blue fin marking was 24 inches wide and 27 inches high. Squadron codes were approximately 18 inches high in Sky. The 18 inch wide rear fuselage band and the de Havilland propeller spinner were also in Sky. The 8 inch high Night serial number was in the usual place on the rear fuselage. Note the presentation name *'Nigeria Ovo Province'* infront of the windscreen.

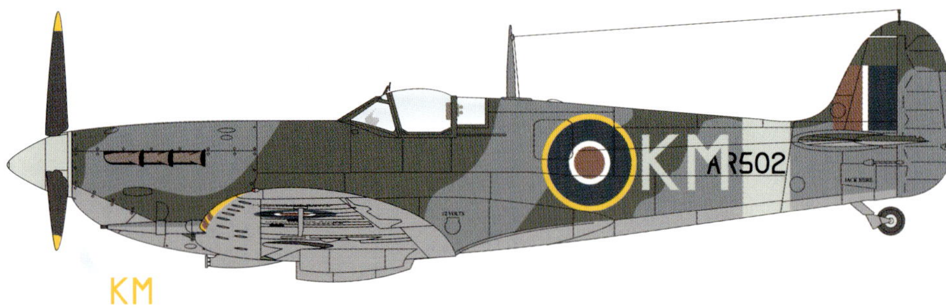

Spitfire Mk Vc, AR502, KM, flown by W/Cdr Karel Mrazak, Czech Wing Leader (Nos 310 and 312 Squadrons), Redhill, August 1942
Karel Mrazak had flown with Nos 43 and 46 Squadrons in 1940, and by the early summer of 1942 had risen to the rank of Wing Commander – allowing him the privilige of carrying his initials on his personal aircraft, an early production Mk Vc. AR502, in which he flew two sorties on 19 August during 'Operation Jubilee', was probably finished in Mixed Grey and Dark Green upper surfaces, (in the A Scheme), with Medium Sea Grey under surfaces. 56 inch diameter Red/Blue National marking I roundels were carried above the wings, with newly-applied 36 inch diameter Red/White/Blue/Yellow National marking III fuselage roundels and 32 inch diameter Red/White/Blue National marking II under wing roundels. The Fin marking (i), was 24 inches wide and 24 inches high. Mrazak's initials were approximately 20 inches high in Sky. The 18 inch wide rear fuselage band and the 'pointed' Rotol propeller were in Sky, and the 8 inch high Night serial number was in the usual place on the rear fuselage. Note Mrazak's initials under the nose in yellow.

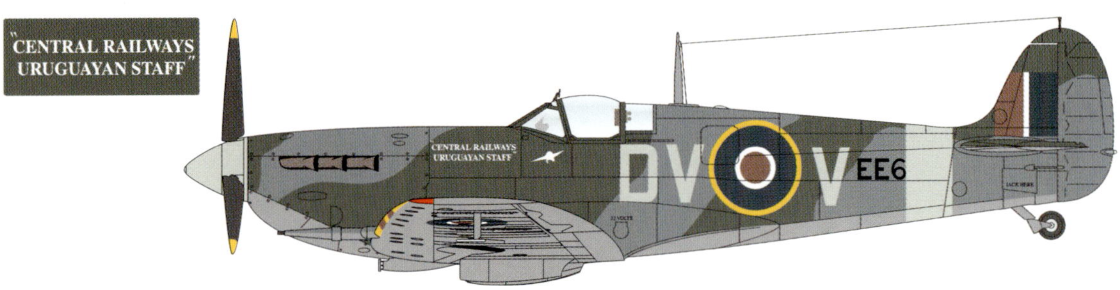

Spitfire Mk Vc, EE602, DV•V of No 129 (Province of Mysore) Squadron, Ibsley, May 1943
EE602 flew with 'clipped' wing tips and was almost certaily finished in the standard Day Fighter Scheme of Ocean Grey and Dark Green upper surfaces, (in the A Scheme), with Medium Sea Grey under surfaces by the time it was on No 129's books. 56 inch diameter Red/Blue National marking I roundels were carried above the wings, with 36 inch diameter Red/White/Blue/Yellow National marking III fuselage roundels and 32 inch diameter Red/White/Blue National marking II under wing roundels. The Fin marking (i), was 24 inches wide and 24 inches high. Squadron codes were approximately 20 inches high in Sky, with the 18 inch wide rear fuselage band and the 'pointed' Rotol propeller spinner also in Sky. The 8 inch high Night serial number was in the usual position but was partially obscured by the rear fuselage band. Note the presentation name *'Central railways Uruguayan Staff'* on the cowling side and the unidentified marking under the windscreen.

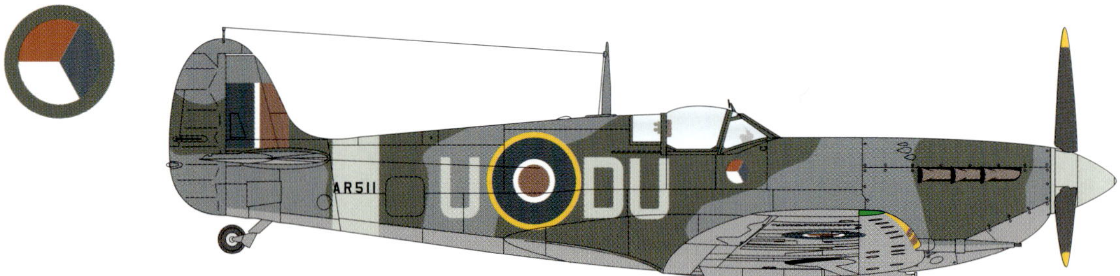

Spitfire Mk Vc, AR511, DU•U of No 312 (Czech) Squadron, Peterhead, July 1943
Another Mk Vc which flew with 'clipped' wing tips, AR511 was finished in the standard Day Fighter Scheme of Ocean Grey and Dark Green upper surfaces, (in the A Scheme), with Medium Sea Grey under surfaces. 56 inch diameter Red/Blue National marking I roundels were carried above the wings, with 36 inch diameter Red/White/Blue/Yellow National marking III fuselage roundels and 32 inch diameter Red/White/Blue National marking II under wing roundels. The Fin marking (i), was 24 inches wide and 24 inches high. Squadron codes were approximately 24 inches high in Sky, with the 18 inch wide rear fuselage band and the 'pointed' Rotol propeller spinner also in Sky. The Night serial number was in the usual position but was smaller being approximately 4 inches high. Note the Czech national marking under the windscreen.

Spitfire Mk.Vc

Spitfire Mk Vc, AR491, NN•D of No 310 (Czech) Squadron, Exeter, August 1943

AR491 is typical of the 'clipped' wing Mk Vcs No 310 Sqn used on Ramrods (ie bomber escorts) over France during the best part of 1942 and 1943 – with just a brief interlude on high flying Mk VIs in Scotland from July to September 1943, (see page 30), before returning south and back Mk Vcs again. AR491 was finished in the standard Day Fighter Scheme of Ocean Grey and Dark Green upper surfaces, (in the A Scheme), with Medium Sea Grey under surfaces. 56 inch diameter Red/Blue National marking I roundels were carried above the wings, with 36 inch diameter Red/White/Blue/Yellow National marking III fuselage roundels and 32 inch diameter Red/White/Blue National marking II under wing roundels. The Fin marking (i), was 24 inches wide and 24 inches high. Squadron codes were approximately 20 inches high in Sky, with the 18 inch wide rear fuselage band and the 'pointed' Rotol propeller spinner also in Sky. The 8 inch high Night serial number was in the usual position across the rear fuselage band but was partially obscured by the Squadron code letters on the starboard side. Note the Czech national marking under both sides of the windscreen.

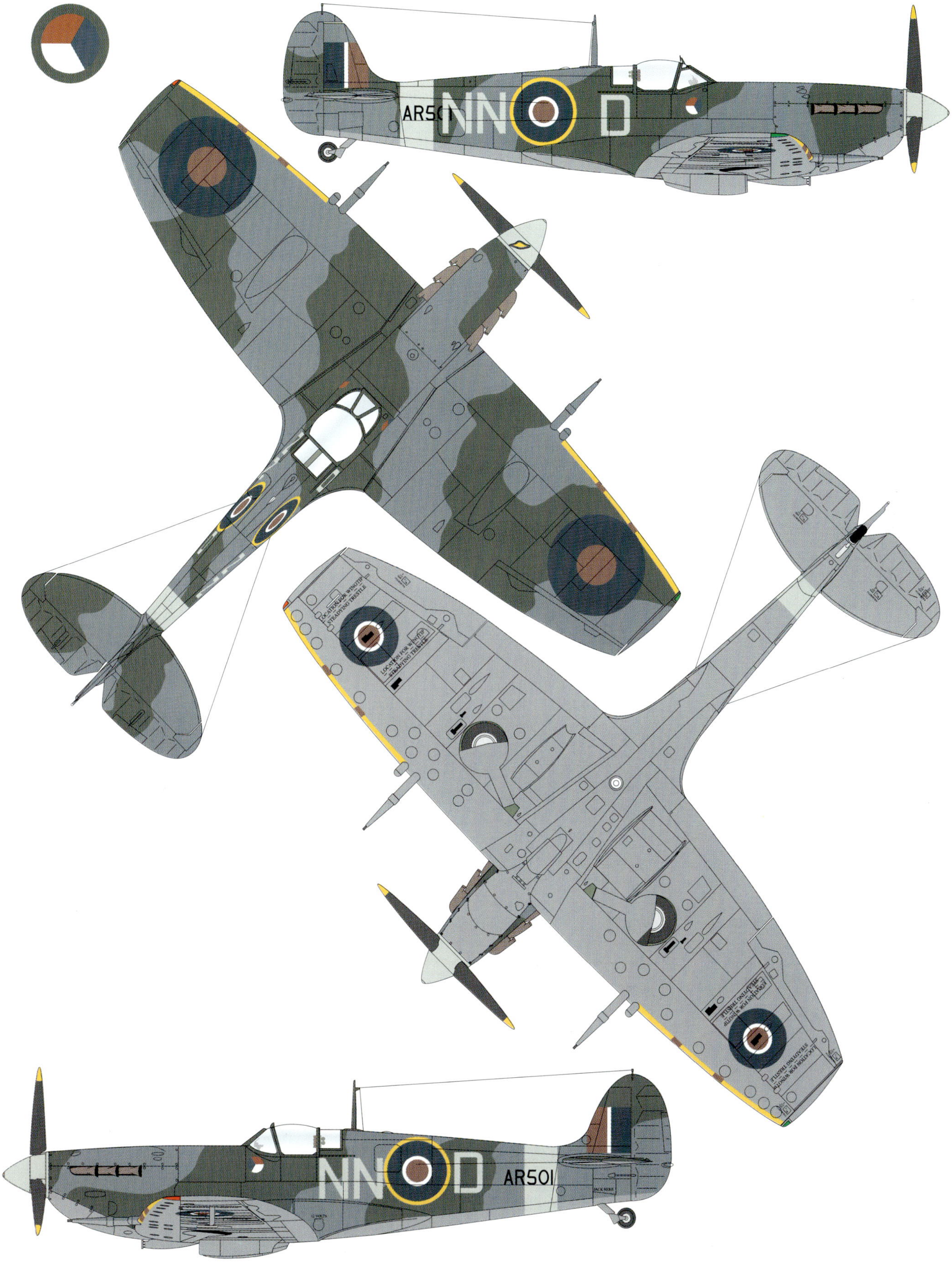

Spitfire Mk.VI

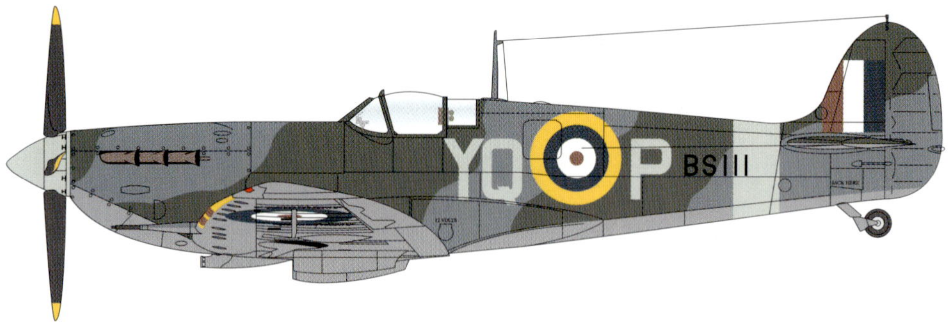

Spitfire HF Mk VI, BS111, YQ•P of No 616 (South Yorkshire) Squadron, West Malling, July/August 1942

BS111 was taken on No 616 Squadron's charge in July 1942, and may well have still been finished in Mixed Grey and Dark Green upper surfaces, (in the A Scheme), with Medium Sea Grey under surfaces. 56 inch diameter Red/Blue roundels were carried above the wings, with 35 inch diameter, Red/White/Blue/Yellow fuselage roundels and 50 inch diameter Red/White/Blue roundels under the wings. The Red/White/Blue fin marking was 24 inches wide and 27 inches high. Squadron codes were approximately 24 inches high in Sky. The 18 inch wide rear fuselage band and the four-bladed Rotol propeller spinner were also in Sky. The 8 inch high Night serial number was in the usual place on the rear fuselage.

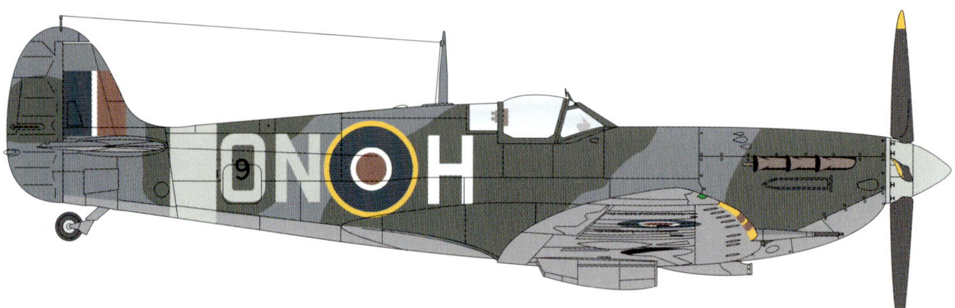

Spitfire HF Mk VI, BR579, ON•H of No 124 (Baroda) Squadron, Gravesend, August 1942, flown by P/O Michael Kilburn

Whilst flying BR579, P/O Kilburn destroyed a Fw 190 during 'Operation Jubilee' on 19 August 1942. BR579 was finished in the standard Day Fighter Scheme of Ocean Grey and Dark Green upper surfaces, (in the A Scheme), and Medium Sea Grey under surfaces. 56 inch diameter Red/Blue National marking I roundels were carried above the wings, with newly applied 36 inch diameter Red/White/Blue/Yellow National marking III fuselage roundels and 32 inch diameter Red/White/Blue National marking II under wing roundels. The Fin marking (i), was 24 inches wide and 24 inches high. Squadron codes were approximately 24 inches high in Sky, although the individual aircraft letter may have been in a lighter shade or even white. The 18 inch wide rear fuselage band and the four-bladed Rotol propeller spinner were also in Sky, with the 8 inch high Night serial number in the usual place on the rear fuselage but almost completely obscured by the rear fuselage band and the Squadron code letters.

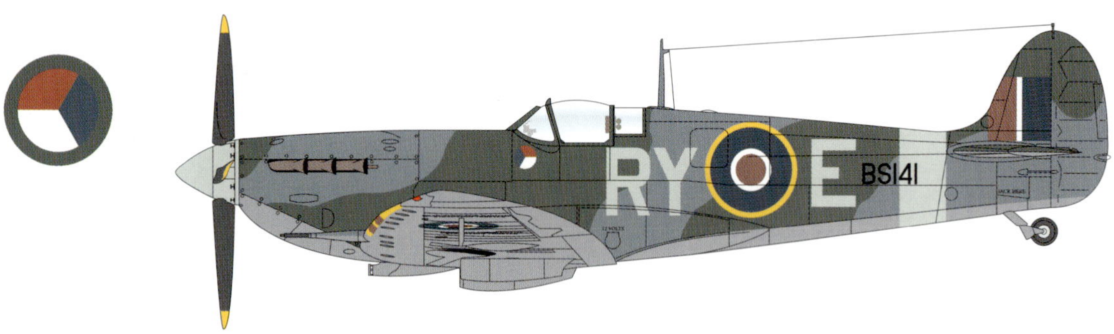

Spitfire HF Mk VI, BS141, RY•E of No 313 (Czech) Squadron, Peterhead, Scotland, June 1943

No 313 Squadron spent a couple of months in Scotland flying the HF Mk VI on high altitude patrols against Luftwaffe photo reconnaissance incursions before being replaced by another Czech-manned unit, No 310, (see below), and returning south to Hawkinge and back on to Mk Vcs . BS141 was finished in the standard Day Fighter Scheme of Ocean Grey and Dark Green upper surfaces, (in the A Scheme), and Medium Sea Grey under surfaces. 56 inch diameter Red/Blue National marking I roundels were carried above the wings, with 36 inch diameter Red/White/Blue/Yellow National marking III fuselage roundels and 32 inch diameter Red/White/Blue National marking II under wing roundels. The Fin marking (i), was 24 inches wide and 24 inches high. Squadron codes were approximately 24 inches high, in Sky, as were the 18 inch wide rear fuselage band and the four-bladed Rotol propeller spinner. The 8 inch high Night serial number was in the usual place on the rear fuselage. Note the Czech national marking under (both sides of) the windscreen.

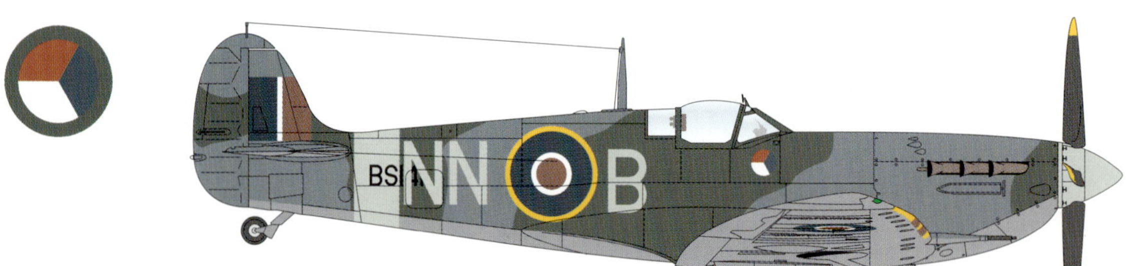

Spitfire HF Mk VI, BS141, NN•B of No 310 (Czech) Squadron, Castletown, Scotland, August/September 1943

No 310 took over No 313 Squadron's HF Mk VIs in July 1943 for a three-month detatchment covering Scapa Flow. This illustration shows BS141 again, (see above), as she looked in No 310 markings, still finished in the standard Day Fighte Scheme of Ocean Grey and Dark Green upper surfaces, (in the A Scheme), and Medium Sea Grey under surfaces. 56 inch diameter Red/Blue National marking I roundels were carried above the wings, with 36 inch diameter Red/White/Blue/Yellow National marking III fuselage roundels and 32 inch diameter Red/White/Blue National marking II under wing roundels. The Fin marking (i), was 24 inches wide and 24 inches high. Squadron codes were approximately 24 inches high, in Sky, as were the 18 inch wide rear fuselage band and the four-bladed Rotol propeller spinner. The 8 inch high Night serial number remained in the usual place on the rear fuselage. Note the Czech national marking, still under (both sides of) the windscreen.

SPITFIRE CAMOUFLAGE AND MARKINGS COLOURS

Dark Green: Introduced in 1936, Dark Green was used as part of the upper surface disruptive camouflage pattern in the Temperate Land Scheme finish with Dark Earth, or the Day Fighter Scheme finish with Mixed Grey or Ocean Grey.
Nearest FS 595B match = 34079

Dark Earth: Introduced in 1936, Dark Earth was used as part of the upper surface disruptive camouflage pattern in the Temperate Land Scheme finish with Dark Green.
Nearest FS 595B match = 30118

Ocean Grey: The exact origins of this colour remain obscure at the time of writing, but it is thought that the name Ocean Grey was originally coined at the RAE towards the end of August 1941. It is not thought to have been generally introduced on the production line until early-1942 and was used as one of the upper surface colours in the Day Fighter Scheme with Dark Green.
Nearest FS 595B match = 36152

Mixed Grey: Upper surface camouflage colour, initially used following the introduction of the Day Fighter Scheme finish in August 1941, pending the introduction of Ocean Grey proper, to be mixed at MUs or on the squadrons by mixing seven parts Medium Sea Grey to one part Night – used as part of the Day Fighter Scheme finish with Dark Green.
Nearest FS 595B match = 36118

Aluminium: Under surface colour, initially used on early production Spitfires – as the Temperate Land Scheme under surface finish until the introduction of Sky.
Nearest FS 595B match = 17178

Night: Introduced in 1937, Night was not a true black as such but a very dark blue-grey. It was used as the covering for the Spitfire's propeller blades and for propeller spinners from 1938 until the introduction of Sky coloured spinners in November 1940. It also featured as the colour in which the serial numbers were applied, on the fuselage sides and under the wings of early Spitfires; as one of the colours in the 'high visibility' Special Recognition Marking under surface scheme with White (and Aluminium). There was also a temporary distemper known as **Special Night**, which was used on the under surface of the port wing of Day Fighters from November 1940 until the re-introduction of overall Sky in mid-April 1941. Nearest FS 595B match = 37030

Sky: Introduced from June 1940, it now appears to have been the middle of September before its use as the main under surface colour of Day Fighters finished in the Temperate Land Scheme was widely established. The variations in under surface colour noted on Spitfires from June 1940 until well in to the autumn are now thought to have been a mixture of 'on Squadron' mixed paint and/or, alternative existing colours supplied to the RAF by paint manufacturers. Sky was also used as the colour for propeller spinners and the 'Fighter Command' rear fuselage band, ostensibly from November 1940, but in practice from about mid-1941. Its other use was for Squadron code letters in conjunction with the Day Fighter Scheme introduced in August 1941. Nearest FS 595B match = 34424

Sky Blue: Introduced from 1939, it was used as the colour for propeller spinners and the 'Fighter Command' rear fuselage band from November 1940, in lieu of Sky, until mid-1941 when Sky spinners and rear fuselage bands became standard.
Nearest FS 595B match = 35550

Medium Sea Grey: In general use from about 1936, it was initially used on Spitfires as the main colour for Squadron code letters in conjunction with the Dark Earth/Dark Green Temperate Land Scheme, and then as the under surface colour for the Ocean Grey/Dark Green Day Fighter Scheme introduced in August 1941.
Nearest FS 595B match = 36270

Red: The dull identification colour used in National markings and code letters.
Nearest FS 595B match = 30109

Blue: The dull identification colour used in National markings.
Nearest FS 595B match = 35048

Yellow: The identification colour used in National markings and along the leading edges of wings in conjunction with the Ocean Grey/Dark Green/Medium Sea Grey Day Fighter Scheme.
Nearest FS 595B match = 33538

White: The identification colour used in National markings, or as one of the colours in the 'high visibility' Special Recognition Marking under surface scheme with Night (and Aluminium).
No FS 595B match

Following the publication of the first two **On Target 'Profiles'** books, (on the ***'Lockheed F-104 in worldwide service' and the 'P-51 Mustang in RAF and Commonwealth service')***, we received some very helpful and constructive suggestions on how to further improve the series. One of the most frequent, was one suggestion asking us to include the reference, upon which the illustration was based, in with the caption. We looked in to this possibility, but eventually concluded that as the captions were already quite long and detailed, (and in some cases 'very long and somewhat involved'), and as many of the illustrations were based upon a mix of more than one reference source, we might better serve the reader if we listed all of the reference sources, used throughout each individual book, on a specific reference list page. So, from now on, all **On Target 'Profiles'** with feature a full list of all the books, (and any other material), consulted during their preparation.

References consulted

'Fighter Squadrons of the RAF and their aircraft' by John D R Rawlings, published by MacDonald & Co, London, 1969

'Spitfire: The History' by Eric B Morgan and Edward Shacklady, published by Key Publishing Ltd., Stamford, 1987

'Spitfire at War' by Alfred Price, published by Ian Allan Ltd., Surrey, 1974

'Spitfire at War: 2' by Alfred Price, published by Guild Publishing Ltd., London, 1985

'Spitfire at War: 3' by Alfred Price, published by Ian Allan Ltd., London, 1989

'The Spitfire Story' by Alfred Price, published by Jane's Publishing Company Ltd., London, 1982

'Spitfire a Documentary History' by Alfred Price, published by MacDonald and Jane's Ltd., London, 1977

'Spitfire Special' by Ted Hooton, published by Ian Allan Ltd., Shepperton, 1972

'Spitfire – the story of a famous fighter' by Bruce Robertson, published by Harleyford Publications Ltd., Hemel Hempstead, 1960

'Spitfire – the Canadians' by Robert Bracken, published by The Boston Mills Press, Canada, 1995

'Spitfire II – the Canadians' by Robert Bracken, published by The Boston Mills Press, Canada, **1999**

'Spitfire Mk I/II Aces 1939-41' Osprey Aircraft of the Aces – 12 by Alfred Price, published by Osprey Publishing, London, 1996

'Spitfire Mk V Aces 1941-45' Osprey Aircraft of the Aces – 16 by Alfred Price, published by Osprey Publishing, London, 1997

'No 91 'Nigeria' Squadron' Osprey Aviation Elite – 3 by Peter Hall, published by Osprey Publishing, Oxford, 2001

'Zumbach's Donalds' Model Detail Photo Monograph No 5, by Wojtek Matusiak, published by Rossagraph, Poland, 2002

'Camouflage & Markings No 1 – Supermarine Spitfire RAF Northern Europe 1936-45', by James Goulding, published by Ducimus Books Ltd., London, 1969

'The Battle for Britain – RAF May to December 1940' Camouflage & Markings No 2, Scale Aircraft Monographs, by Paul Lucas, published by Guideline Publications Ltd., Luton, 2000

'Spitfire – Fighter Supreme' by Alfred Price, published by Arms and Armour Press, London, 1991

'Spitfire – in action' by Jerry Scutts, published by Squadron/Signal Publications, Texas, 1980

'Spitfire – Classic Aircraft No 1' by Roy Cross and Gerald Scarborough, published by Patrick Stephens Ltd., London, 1971

'British Fighters of World War Two – Vol 1' by Francis K Mason, published by Hylton Lacy Publishers Ltd., Berkshire, 1969

'Archive – Supermarine Spitfire Mk I' by Peter Moss, published by Container Publications Ltd., Oxford, 1975

'Supermarine Spitfire Remembered' by Philip J R Moyes, published by Wingspan Publications, Oxford, 1975

'Supermarine Spitfire I & II' Aerodata International No 2, by Philip J R Moyes, published by Vintage Aviation Publications Ltd, Oxford, 1977

'Supermarine Spitfire Mk I-XVI in RAF and Foreign Service' Aircam Aviation Series No 4, by Ted Hooton and Richard Ward, published by Osprey Publishing Ltd., Kent, 1968

'Supermarine Spitfire I & II' Profile Publications No 41, by Philip J R Moyes, published by Profile Publications Ltd., Surrey, 1965

'Supermarine Spitfire V series' Profile Publications No 166, by Ted Hooton, published by Profile Publications Ltd., Surrey, 1967

'Fighter Command 1939-45' by Ian Carter, published by Ian Allan Publishing Ltd., Surrey, 2002

'Spitfire Mk V in action' by Peter Caygill, published by Airlife Publishing Ltd., Shrewsbury, 2001

'The Darlington Spitfire', by Peter Caygill, published by Airlife Publishing Ltd., Shrewsbury, 1999

'The Spitfire – 50 years on', by Michael J F Bowyer, published by Patrick Stephens Ltd., Wellingborough, 1986

'Spitfire – the combat history', by Robert Jackson, published by Airlife Publishing Ltd., Shrewsbury, 1995

'American Eagles – American volunteers in the RAF 1937 – 1943' Classic Colours, by Tony Holmes, published by Classic Publications, East Sussex, 2001

'RAAF fighters over the UK', Air Extra No 4, edited by Philip J R Moyes, published by Ian Allan Ltd., Shepperton, 1974

'Aircraft for the Few - the RAF's Fighters and Bombers in 1940', by Michael J F Bowyer, published by Patrick Stephens Ltd., Yeovil, 1991

'Fighting Colours: RAF fighter camouflage and markings 1937 – 1975', by Michael J F Bowyer, published by Patrick Stephens Ltd., Cambridge, 1969

'The Greatest Air Battle – Dieppe 19 August 1942', by Norman Franks, published by Grub Street, London, 1992

'The Squadrons of the Royal Air Force', by James J Halley, published by Air-Britain (Historians) Ltd., Kent, 1980

'Squadron Codes 1937-56', by Michael J F Bowyer and John D R Rawlings, published by Patrick Stephens Ltd., Cambridge, 1979

'Combat Codes', by Vic Flintham and Andrew Thomas, published by Airlife Publishing Ltd., Shrewsbury, 2003

'RAF Squadrons', by C G Jefford, published by Airlife Publishing Ltd., Shrewsbury, 1998

'Royal Air Force Aircraft – serial numbers', by James J Halley, published by Air-Britain (Historians) Ltd., Kent

K1000 to K9999 (1976)

L1000 to L9999 (1979)

N1000 to N9999 (1977)

P1000 to P9999 (1978)

R1000 to R9999 (1980)

V1000 to V9999/W1000 to W9999 (1983)

X1000 to X9999/Z1000 to Z9999 (1984)

AA100 to AZ999 (1985)

'Spitfire – Supermarine Spitfire Mk V' Aeroguide Classics No 1, by Roger Chesneau, published by Linewrights Ltd, Essex, 1985

'Supermarine Spitfire Mk V' No 1/ Vol IV, edited by Nakladatelstvi Zlinek, published by Zlinek Publications, Czech Republic, 1992

'The Spitfire Mk V Manual' RAF Museum Series, edited by Michael A Fopp, published by Greenhill Books, London, 2003

'Supermarine Spitfire' by Peter Moss, published by Ducimus Books Ltd., London, 1970

'In Enemy Hands' by Bryan Philpott, published by Patrick Stephens Ltd., Cambridge, 1981

...and with special thanks to:–

Paul Lucas, for his encyclopaedic knowledge of RAF colour schemes and markings and his willingness to share it, and Ian Carter, Alan Wakefield and Janice Mullin of the Imperial War Museum, for access to their Photographic Archive Department.